The naval front

Gordon S Maxwell, Donald Maxwell

THE NAVAL FRONT

OTHER WAR FRONTS

A NIGHT IMPRESSION OF THE NAVY HOUSE,
BAGHDAD, FEBRUARY 1919

By the courtesy of the Imperial War Museum

BY GORDON S. MAXWELL
LIEUT. R.N.V.R.

ILLUSTRATED IN
COLOUR & MONOCHROME

BY DONALD MAXWELL
LIEUT. R.N.V.R.

A. & C. BLACK, LIMITED
SOHO SQUARE, LONDON, W.1

TO MY MOTHER

PUBLISHERS' NOTE

A FEW words of introduction about the two brothers who produced this book may be of interest.

The elder, Lieut. Donald Maxwell, was well-known before the War as a naval artist on the staff of *The Graphic*. During the War he served in the R.N.V.R. on a North Sea Patrol and later with the Sheerness Naval Forces in command of H.M.M.L. 139. In 1918 he was appointed Admiralty Official Artist, and went out to Mesopotamia and Palestine to do pictures for the Imperial War Museum, which resulted in the making of a good many of the sketches in this book, and also in two other books of which he is both author and artist—*The Last Crusade* and *A Dweller in Mesopotamia*. In pre-war days he was a keen yachtsman and traveller, as he has shown in his books *The Log of the Griffin*, *A Cruise across Europe*, and *Adventures with a Sketch-Book*.

Lieut. Gordon S. Maxwell also served in the R.N.V.R. during the War : in the North Sea, The Dover Patrol, and Dunkirk. He was mentioned in Despatches at the Zeebrugge Raid in April, 1918, when he was in command of H.M. M.L. 314. He was subsequently appointed Commanding Officer of the flotilla of M.L.s from the Dover Patrol sent to Harwich to assist in the surrender of the U-Boats. He is known in naval circles for his book of humorous verse *The Rhymes of a Motor Launch* and his longer prose book *The Motor Launch Patrol*, the latter also being illustrated by his brother, whom he accompanied in pre-war days on many of his yachting cruises and rambles abroad.

The Publishers wish to thank the Art Committee of the Imperial War Museum and the Editor of *The Graphic* for their courtesy in allowing certain pictures in their possession to be reproduced in this book.

A. & C. BLACK.

CONTENTS

CHAPTER I

x CONTENTS

CHAPTER VIII

CHAPTER IX

CHAPTER X

CHAPTER XI

CHAPTER XII

CHAPTER XIII

CHAPTER XIV

LIST OF ILLUSTRATIONS

In Colour

THE NAVAL FRONT.

CHAPTER I.

WATCH AND WARD.

WHEN one considers that the Front held by the British Navy during their increasing watch throughout the war includes practically every square mile of the Seven Seas, it will be seen how impossible it is to encompass all the deeds of such a force into a single volume; it would require a library of naval books to tell of every patrol and all that befel upon it, for to quote the words of the Prime Minister, when speaking of Naval Patrols: " Their work and peril never ends, and their hardships and dangers are barely realised. But through their actions security and plenty are enjoyed by the population of these islands. They patrol the seas from the icy waters of the Arctic Ocean to the stormy flood of Magellan.

" There is not an ocean, a sea, a bay, a gulf, there is not an estuary used for commerce which is not patrolled by the ships of the British Navy.

A

How dangerous a task it is the casualty lists proclaim, because in proportion to their numbers the dead are equal to those of the British Army. Through it all the command of the sea has been maintained." So my aim in this book will be to describe the more salient points, incidents that have had a marked effect upon the naval situation and have taken and retained a strong hold upon the public imagination.

Save for certain climatic differences and making due allowance for environment, one patrol is very much like another, especially in the North Sea : the same deadly monotony and the same weary watches. It has been said, and very truly, that it was the long and weary watches of the British Navy that won the war ; and this sums up the work of the Navy very aptly, for quite three-quarters of a sailor's life in war time is spent on watching and waiting, in this particular war for an enemy who seldom ventured to show his nose outside harbour. The other quarter is fierce excitement.

But though wearisome, and often monotonous, as are the long days at sea, a sailor has to face and fight a still greater power than that of the enemy—the elements ; fighting his way often in

THE MIRROR BY NIGHT MINELAYER *PRINCESS MARGARET* STARTING ON A NIGHT JOB

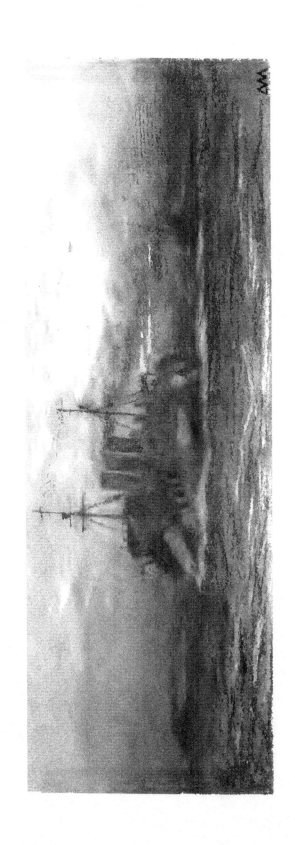

the teeth of a gale on some appointed task or enveloped in his still worse foe, a fog.

Night patrol is another matter, for though perhaps more wearisome still, it possesses even greater possibilities of the unknown, when every shadow ahead may hold a foe, or every wave wash a mine against the bows of the ship. In fact, life on patrol may be compared to that of a policeman or a fireman, full of long waits, with possibilities of sudden perils and thrills. There is no finer or more efficient section of the Navy than those ships to whom has fallen the work of maintaining, to a very large extent, these patrols. I mean the various flotillas of H.M. Destroyers and Light Cruiser squadrons.

At the same time the work of the Auxiliary Patrol, a force which only came into being under war conditions, cannot be overlooked, for they were responsible for quite three-quarters of the coastal patrols round the British Isles and in the Mediterranean ; so perhaps it will be as well, in passing, to speak of the work of these vessels, who helped to keep the coastal front, before we get on to the deeds of the bigger ships in more distant waters.

The Auxiliary Patrol was a heterogeneous

force, composed of all sorts of conditions of vessels, some pressed into service from more peaceful pursuits, and some built specially for the work. Of the former the lion's share of the work fell to the trawlers and drifters who were run by R.N.R. officers and manned for the most part by men who had already served· on them as fishermen. There is no doubt that we owe much in this war to our adaptability to any conditions that may come along, and no better example of this can be found than these men, and to the officers and men of the R.N.V.R., whose accomplishments after but short training show very clearly how deeply the sea-love of our island race is ingrained in its men. It was our fathers whose deeds on the sea made England what she is, and we are proud to think that their sons have carried on this glorious tradition, and in its hour of need their country did not find them wanting.

It was these trawlers that also did nearly all the mine-sweeping; they were the housemaids of the ocean, and well they did their dangerous work, keeping the trade routes and war channels clear alike for merchant vessels and H.M. ships, and to the drifters fell the task of laying and guarding the long lines of anti-submarine nets. What the Royal Navy think of these " amateurs " is perhaps best expressed in the words of an R.N. Captain. " They're absolutely It," he said, " no weather seems too bad for them. They're our eyes and ears. They know every wave in the channel, not merely as passing acquaintances, but by their Christian names ! They'll do anything, go anywhere and chance the luck. They're just simple fishermen, but they run the whole show magnificently—guns, semaphores, wireless, everything ! They live on kippers and tea, and I don't believe they ever go to sleep ! "

For mine-sweeping all sorts of vessels were employed as well as trawlers, and not a few ships that began their careers as pleasure steamers ended them gloriously under the White Ensign. It would be interesting to know (though to get at such figures is naturally an utter impossibility), how many lives these mine-sweepers have saved by clearing away the Death that Floats from the trade-routes and fairways round the coasts, not only of Britain, but in many another part of the world.

Of the men who manned these boats Mr. Lloyd George said in one of his speeches : " I would like to say a word about our fishermen. Their contribution has been a great one. Sixty per cent. of our fishermen are in the naval service. Their trawlers are engaged in some of the most perilous tasks that can be entrusted to sailors— mine-sweeping, a dangerous occupation often ending in disaster. The number of mines that they have swept up is incredible, and if they had not done this Britain would now have been blockaded by a ring of deadly machines anchored round her shores. But their service has not been confined to this work. You find their trawlers patrolling the seas everywhere, pro- tecting ships, not merely around the British Isles. You find these fishing trawlers in the Mediterranean. They surely deserve the best thanks that we can accord them for the services they have rendered."

Types of vessels, too, have been employed in this war, that were never thought likely to be used in warfare. The motor launches, built in America for use in the Royal Navy, were an example of these, manned by officers of the R.N.V.R. and men of the special Trawler Reserve. Varied have been their duties on different patrols; and the coastal motor boats, smaller and faster

H M. TRANSPORTS *EKMA* AND *ELEPHANTA* A l
SUEZ

By the courtesy of the Imperial War Muse um

still, have all gone to make up the force which lay behind all the greater activities which the Royal Navy carried out with the larger ships.

Sir Edward Carson, in a speech, said of this extra strain suddenly put upon the nation's maritime resources : " You have a war—a naval war—going on over the whole of the seas—war in the Channel, war in the Atlantic, war in the Pacific, war in the Mediterranean, war round Egypt, war in the Adriatic, war in Mesopotamia, war at Salonika, and day by day the Navy is called upon to supply the material for carrying on all these wars. Did anybody ever contemplate war of that kind ? When I mention one figure to you, that at the commencement of the war we had something like 150 small vessels for patrol work, and now we have something like 3000, you will see the gigantic feat that has been accomplished by the Navy. In all these theatres of war we have to provide patrols, convoys, mine-sweepers, mine-layers, air service, mine carriers and fleet messengers."

There is nothing showy about patrol work, and little save passing references appear in the press about this duty (for obvious reasons in war time), but nevertheless it can be counted

among the most strenuous and nerve-racking
tasks imaginable; especially in a small boat in
winter, when rough, tumbling seas are continu-
ally breaking over the bows as the ship staggers
up from the hollow of one wave but to plunge
into the one ahead, climbing up the oncoming
mountain of water into the smothering crest,
when she seems to shake herself like a dog as
she plunges down once again, with streaming
decks, into the next hollow, and so on for hour
after hour. But the raging sea and wild sky
are old acquaintances to the fishermen-sailors,
and the tough little boat, rolling and pitching
like a thing possessed, was his home for years
before the Germans came to disturb his trade;
though he still pursues his old calling with a
change of quarry.

Many tales could be told of the encounters
of these trawlers and drifters with enemy submarines if space allowed it; there is that of
the trawler *Commissioner*, who met a U-Boat in
the North Sea and whose skipper made the
laconic, but pointed, report: "Our first shot
missed the submarine, so did our second, the
third hit the enemy's conning tower, the fourth
hit the enemy's gun, and the fifth sent the

"OUR FATHERS HAVE TOLD US"

Milestones in Naval History.

From the picture exhibited at the Royal Academy, 1918.

submarine down in flames, and all was over, bar the shouting."

Then there was the drifter *Gowanlee*, who, when summoned to surrender by an Austrian cruiser in the Adriatic, told the enemy ship that she "would see 'em in hell first," and then opened fire on the cruiser with a six-pounder and actually made good her escape from their powerful adversary.

So with these few remarks about the "Fleet behind the Fleet," a curtain lifter, as it were, to the scene played on wider stage occupied by the Royal Navy proper, we can draw the curtain to show the great drama of sea-power, but let it not be forgotten that it was the work of these smaller and humbler auxiliary craft in doing the "odd jobs" of the sea, that freed the other ships from this duty, and enabled them to hold the seas of the world for those long and weary years in a grip which never loosened, to watch with unsleeping eyes, and when the time came to hit—and hit hard.

CHAPTER II.

TWO GERMAN RAIDERS AND THEIR FATE.

THE destruction of the two German raiders *Emden* and *Königsberg* is typical of that which befell all German warships that were not in home waters at the outbreak of war.

Of these two the former was the first to go, and the doings of His Imperial Germanic Majesty's ship *Emden*—to give her the full title she bore at the time—and its destruction by H.M.S. *Sydney* form a short, but very vivid, chapter of Naval History.

The German cruiser in her various ingenious disguises had been raiding merchant ships in the Pacific, and had been clever enough to evade capture for some time. It had not been a case of " spurlos versenkt " this time, for the *Emden's* captain was an exception to most German commanders in his treatment of the crews of the ships he sank. He gave warning of his intention, and took the men aboard his own ship, or placed them on one of the captured vessels on which he had put a prize crew.

His time was drawing short, however, for on a morning early in November, 1914, a convoy of ships that were being escorted by the *Melbourne* and the *Sydney* received a wireless message from Cocos to say that a foreign warship was off the harbour entrance there. The *Sydney* at once went off to investigate. This was just as it was getting light, about seven a.m., and after steaming for about two hours she sighted land ahead and soon after saw the smoke of a ship, which proved to be the *Emden*. She was advancing at a very rapid rate, probably with the idea of escaping before the British ship got near the spot she had been, but when she saw that there was no chance of doing this she showed fight and was the first to open fire. Her guns, however, were outranged by those of the *Sydney*, but the enemy continued to close, and upon getting his own range his shooting was accurate and rapid at first, but seemed to fall off after the two or three broadsides, nearly all the casualties on the British ship occurring in the first few minutes of the fight. Then the superior marksmanship and cooler fighting of our men began to tell, and the

Emden came in for some very rough handling. Her foremost funnel was shot away, and soon after her mainmast also. She was holed in several places, and a fire was seen to break out aft. Her second funnel was the next to go, and lastly the third. She was in a very bad way, and making water so rapidly that she was forced to make in-shore as fast as her damaged condition would allow.

North Keeling Island was the nearest land at the time, and it was for the beach here that she was making. The *Sydney* gave her two more broadsides as she closed to pursue, and the *Emden* soon after grounded. The action had taken just over an hour and a half, and during the later part of this time the *Sydney* had observed a merchant ship that was cruising about in the vicinity in rather a mysterious fashion. Guns were trained on her but not fired, but as soon as the *Emden* was driven ashore the new-comer made off as fast as she could. The main quarry now being safe from escape the *Sydney* gave pursuit, and soon overhauled the merchantman and fired two shots across her bows as a signal to stop, which she did. An armed party was sent aboard, and she proved to be S.S. *Buresk,* a British Collier that had been captured by the *Emden*, which had put a prize crew aboard her.

Unfortunately she was sinking, for as soon as the Germans saw that capture was inevitable they had knocked the sea-cocks in and damaged them beyond repair. All hands were taken aboard the *Sydney*, and four shells were put into the *Buresk*, sinking her at once.

Arriving again off North Keeling Island the *Sydney* found that the *Emden* still had her colours flying. Captain Glossop, who was in command of the British ship, sent her a signal in International Code—" Do you surrender ? "

The *Emden* replied by Morse, " What is the signal ? We have no signal books."

" Do you surrender ? " was then again made in Morse, to which the enemy did not reply. After a short time another signal, " Have you got my signal ? " was sent, but again no reply was received.

The captured German officers from the *Buresk* told the *Sydney's* captain, that von Muller (who was in command of the *Emden*) would never surrender, and this idea was certainly borne out by the dogged silence from the stranded ship, so fire was, very reluctantly, opened on her once more. This had the desired effect, as she showed white flags after two or three shots, and hauled down her ensign.

The prize crew from the *Buresk* was put aboard, and the *Emden* was left for the night. Escape was out of the question, for she was well ashore, and this course was necessary to allow the *Sydney* to discover what damage the raiders had done to the cables and wireless station at Direction Island, which place they were known to have visited, and from where communication had been cut off for some time. It was found that the wireless plant had been completely destroyed, the cable cut, as had been feared.

The next morning the *Sydney* returned to the wrecked ship, taking with her a doctor and two sick-berth ratings to help in giving attention to the German wounded. The state of the *Emden* was beyond description; it was a shambles of dead and dying, and a mass of twisted iron. Her deck was torn up in great gashes, and all her funnels were either blown overboard or lying among the débris. The work of trans-shipping the wounded was a difficult one, owing to the ship being on the weather side of the island, but this was done successfully. About twenty Germans had managed to get ashore, and for these a stretcher party was sent. The wounded shipped, the problem arose as to the disposal of the rest of the *Emden's* crew; it was impossible to leave them where they were, and there was very little accommodation for such a surplus of men on the *Sydney*; but it was decided eventually that if the captain of the German ship would give an undertaking that they would cause no disturbance, and be amenable to the ship's discipline, they should be brought aboard the *Sydney* and looked after as well as might be possible under existing conditions.

This assurance von Muller gave, and it was faithfully kept, though as a matter of fact there was little fight left in the poor devils by this time, after their gruelling of the previous day and such a night as they had spent on the wrecked and battered hulk.

These men were eventually landed at Colombo, though not before several had died of wounds on the voyage. There were just over two hundred prisoners on board altogether, of whom nearly half were wounded; besides this the enemy had had a hundred and fifteen killed in the action.

The casualties of the *Sydney* were very small

in comparison, four killed and twelve wounded.
The damage to the ship had been small too,
only about ten shots had struck her, and these
had only damaged the upper works; not one
shot had been anything like vital to the working
of the ship, the funnels were intact and also the
engine rooms and boilers, which fact, when
compared with the battered mass of metal that
had once been the famous German cruiser *Emden*,
speaks volumes for British naval marksmanship.

The destruction of the *Konigsberg* took place
in July, 1915, after she had taken refuge up the
Rufiji River, in what was once German East
Africa. Here she was spotted by our aeroplanes,
in spite of the fact that she had camouflaged
herself with palm trees and other vegetation in
the hope of escaping notice.

On July 6th a British force, under Vice-Admiral
Sir H. King Hall, attacked her; the monitors
Severn and *Mersey* proceeded across the bar at
the river mouth and cast anchor. From this
position they opened fire on the *Konigsberg*, to
which the German ship replied briskly. The
spotting for the monitors was done by two
aeroplanes, which also dropped bombs on the
German vessel to distract her as much as possible

A little ship was on the sea.

"Our brave sailors then opened fire" *extract from Official*

When suddenly a Hun arose

The result.

Taking the submarine's victim in tow.

A destroyer to the rescue.

The Chase.

"The dog it was that died."

AN EPIC OF THE SEA

As depicted in a page from a Naval Officer's sketch book.

in engaging our ships, upon which fire was also opened from the shore, but a few rounds from the light cruiser *Weymouth* (flying the Admiral's Flag) which replied with her six-inch guns, soon put a stop to this, although it was impossible to locate the exact position of the shore guns owing to their being concealed amongst the trees and the thick undergrowth. From the same cause it was very difficult for the observers in the aeroplanes to mark the falls of the shots of the monitors' guns. For this reason the monitors subsequently moved further up the river, until the tops of the *Königsberg's* masts were visible.

Here the bombardment began afresh, both sides keeping up a very fierce fire, and this battle, which had begun in the early morning, continued until about 2.30 p.m., when the *Konigsberg's* firing had been reduced to one gun. Soon after this the monitors ceased fire and retired out of the river, being again attacked as they did so by the small guns from the shore. The *Severn* luckily escaped without casualties, but the *Mersey* had six men killed and two wounded, and one of her forward guns was put out of action.

" As it was necessary," wrote Admiral King Hall in his despatch, " to make a fresh attack on the *Konigsberg* to complete her destruction, further operations were carried out on July 11th, by which date the aeroplanes were again ready for service, and the monitors had made good certain defects and completed with coal. The attack was carried out on the same lines as on the previous occasion, and the monitors crossed the bar followed by the *Weymouth* and the *Pyramus*, the latter proceeding up the river and searching the banks for concealed gun positions."

On this occasion the monitors were moored about a thousand yards closer to the enemy than on the previous operations, which naturally made their fire more effective. By excellent spotting the aeroplanes soon got the guns on the target, and many hits were signalled. Soon it was reported the *Königsberg* was on fire, when the monitors moved up closer still and completed the destruction of the doomed German ship, which had by this time long since ceased offering any resistance.

When the monitors withdrew the *Kònigsberg* was a complete wreck, having suffered not only from the effect of shells and fire, but also from several explosions, which had been observed by the attackers.

Thus another German commerce raider was sent to her last account, and the credit of this was very largely due to Captain E. J. A. Fullerton of the *Severn*, and Commander R. A. Wilson of the *Mersey*, who carried out a very difficult task, that of entering a river, of which only imperfect knowledge was obtainable, against an unknown invisible defence, with such marked success.

CHAPTER III.

THE BRITISH SUBMARINES AND THE HELIGOLAND BIGHT ACTION.

THE Battle of Heligoland Bight on August 28th, 1914, was the first chance in the war that our submarines had to prove their worth; a worth which has since become famous, now that their fine work, done in secret, has come to light.

The object of the attack upon the Bight was to draw the enemy into action by means of decoys, which in this case were to be eight submarines and two destroyers, and roughly the plan of attack was for these vessels to enter into enemy waters at night, and at dawn show themselves to draw the Germans in pursuit, and incidentally into the range of a flotilla of our destroyers, with whom were the two light cruisers *Arethusa* and *Fearless*, while waiting hull down on the horizon, ready to steam to the attack on instant signal, were the Light Cruiser and Battle Cruiser Squadrons.

Such an operation as this naturally called for careful thought in the preparation, and before such plans could be properly formed information was required that could only be obtained in enemy waters in the Bight itself, and to trace how this was done it will be necessary to look backward a little, for such information must of necessity be gathered in small doses.

The man to whose organising ability the credit for this is due is undoubtedly Vice-Admiral Sir Roger Keyes, in the early days of the war Commodore (S) of the Eighth Submarine Flotilla at Harwich, while to the officers and men serving under him equal credit is due for the way these orders were carried out.

In an early dispatch Vice-Admiral Keyes says, " Three hours after the outbreak of war, Submarines *E* 6 (Lieut.-Commander C. P. Talbot) and *E* 8 (Lieut.-Commander F. H. H. Goodhart), proceeded unaccompanied to carry out a reconnaissance in the Heligoland Bight. These two vessels returned with useful information, and had the privilege of being the pioneers on a service which is attended by some risk.

" During the transportation of the Expeditionary Force the *Lurcher* and the *Firedrake* and all the submarines of the Eighth Submarine Flotilla occupied positions from which they could have attacked the High Sea Fleet had it emerged to dispute the passage of our transports. This patrol was maintained day and night without relief, until the personnel of our Army had been transported and all chance of effective interference had disappeared.

" These submarines have since been incessantly employed on the enemy's coast in the Heligoland Bight and elsewhere, and have obtained much valuable information regarding the composition and movements of his patrols. They have occupied his waters and reconnoitred his anchorages, and, while so engaged, have been subjected to skilful and well executed anti-submarine tactics ; hunted for hours at a time by torpedo craft and attacked by gunfire and torpedoes."

These are modest words, and tell their story plainly and simply, but we can read between the lines and imagine what these patrols were like. The submarines were of an early type, as compared with those with which we finished the war, and their vigil lay in enemy waters, for the most part, to which fresh minefields were constantly being added.

A BIT OF YARMOUTH IN THE EAST   VIEW FROM
QUAY AT NAVY HOUSE, PORT SAID

By the courtesy of the Imperial War Museum

All through the war our submarines have had a splendid record of work well done, and the names of some of the best-known commanders of these vessels come naturally to the mind. Commander Max Horton, who sank the German cruiser *Hela* and the destroyer S 126 in E 19, and Captain Cromie, whose fine work in the Baltic resulted in his sinking ten German transports and the cruiser *Undine*. It was this officer who was subsequently murdered by the Bolshevists in Petrograd.

Some of the finest of our submarine achievements took place in the Mediterranean, when Lieut.-Commander Norman Holbrook won the V.C. for diving under the Turkish minefield in the Dardanelles, torpedoing the battleship *Messudiyeh* in B 11, and Lieut. Nasmith, who actually engaged a detachment of Turkish cavalry in E 11 after the same perilous passage on his way to Constantinople harbour, which he entered and sank a transport, for which he, too, was awarded the V.C. Another wonderful achievement in these waters was that of Lieut. D'Oyly Hughes, of E 14, who blew up a viaduct over the Osmid Railway after swimming ashore in the Sea of Marmora, and making his way through a Turkish farmyard past the enemy sentries. These doings read like those of a boy's adventure book as much as actual happenings, and writers in the future will have a fund of truth to draw upon that will surpass any fictitious account ever written.

When the war with the Turks was at its height, during the operations off the Dardanelles, our submarines, alone, had the wonderful record of sinking or destroying two Turkish battleships, five gunboats, one torpedo boat, eight transports and one hundred and ninety seven supply ships of various sorts.

To return to the action at Heligoland Bight. The submarines at this operation were under the personal command of Admiral Keyes, who set out at midnight on August 26th on board the destroyer *Lurcher*, with the *Firedrake* and eight submarines accompanying him—the $D\,2$, $D\,8$, $E\,4$, $E\,5$, $E\,6$, $E\,7$, $E\,8$, and $E\,9$. No attack was made on that day, but by the evening all was in readiness, the submarines had all reached their appointed billets, the *Arethusa* under Commodore Tyrwhitt, the *Fearless* and two flotillas of destroyers were standing by, while Admiral Beatty in the *Lion* was also near with the Light Cruisers and Battle Cruisers as we have already seen.

EIGHT BELLS, MIDNIGHT

Interior of a British Submarine resting on the bottom of the sea.

Nothing happened during the night, and no sign of the proximity of the British ships was discovered by the enemy, and at dawn three of our submarines, *E* 6, *E* 7 and *E* 8, proceeded on the surface towards Heligoland with the purpose of drawing the enemy, while the *Lurcher* and *Firedrake* made a thorough search of the waters through which our cruisers were to advance to the attack, but finding it clear of hostile submarines followed the decoy boats on their perilous mission.

This had the desired effect, for a division of German destroyers, which were on patrol in the Bight, discovered the British ships and opened fire on them. The *Arethusa* and the Third Destroyer Flotilla coming up to the attack at full speed at once engaged them, and a fierce fight began. Before long there appeared out of the mist—for the morning was a foggy one—two German cruisers, which at once opened fire at our ships. The odds were heavily on the enemy, and the *Arethusa* was hit repeatedly, but a more gallant fight was never put up by any ship than that waged by the " saucy Arethusa " that day. Most of the enemy's fire was directed on her, but she fought on till all her guns were put out of action but one, and this one but a 6-inch, and it was with this solitary gun still spitting defiance at the enemy that the *Fearless* found her, and Captain Blunt, her commanding officer, at once engaged the two German cruisers, and so fierce was his onslaught that they were forced to desist from their attack on the *Arethusa* to defend themselves against this new adversary, which enabled the *Arethusa* to withdraw in a running fight, to take stock of her wounds and patch herself up a bit.

The first flotilla of destroyers were now also in action, and were successful in sinking a German destroyer—*V* 187—which was flying the flag of the German commodore. After this had been done two British destroyers, the *Goshawk* and the *Defender*, both lowered boats to pick up German survivors, and these boats were actually attacked, while engaged on this act of mercy, by a German cruiser which was approaching. The war was yet young in those days, and such an act was thought impossible, but since then we have got to learn that no act can be too low or beastly for the Hun navy to perpetrate. These two boats would undoubtedly have both been sunk had it not been for the pluck and resource of Lieut.-Commander E. W. Leir in submarine *E* 4, whose conduct to the German survivors comes as a very sharp contrast to the dastardly methods of the enemy cruiser.

This act is perhaps best described in Admiral Keyes' own words. He says," Lieut.-Commander E. W. Leir in submarine *E* 4 witnessed the sinking of the German Torpedo Boat Destroyer *V* 187 through his periscope, and, observing a Cruiser of the *Stettin* class close, and open fire on the British destroyers which had lowered their boats to pick up the survivors, he proceeded to attack the cruiser, but she altered course before he could get within range. After covering the retirement of our destroyers, which had had to abandon their boats, he returned to the latter, and embarked a Lieutenant and nine men, of *Defender*, who had been left behind. The boats also contained two officers and eight men of *V* 187 who were unwounded, and eighteen men who were badly wounded. As he could not embark the latter, Lieut.-Commander Leir left one of the officers and six unwounded men to navigate the British boats to Heligoland. Before leaving he saw that they were provided with water, biscuit, and a compass. One

German officer and two men were made prisoners
of war.

" Lieut.-Commander Leir's action in remaining
on the surface in the vicinity of the enemy and
in a visibility which would have placed his
vessel within easy gun range of an enemy appear-
ing out of the mist was altogether admirable."

All through the action the destroyers had been
busy, some of them coming in for rough treatment
at the hands of the larger German ships, especially the *Laurel*, who at one time was engaged
single-handed with three enemy ships, a cruiser
and two destroyers, and succeeded in sinking
one of the latter before help arrived. Her
Commanding officer, Commander F. F. Rose,
continued to fight his ship after being wounded
in both legs, till exhaustion forced him to give
in, when his First Lieutenant, Lieut. C. R. Peploe,
navigated the ship back to port after the action,
in spite of her badly damaged condition.

Meanwhile the *Arethusa* had been busy carrying out repairs and soon had all her guns but
two in working order again. Accordingly, she
returned to the fight, and it was not long before
she came upon a German cruiser, which she at
once engaged.

" We received a very severe and almost accurate fire from this cruiser," wrote Commodore Tyrwhitt after the action, " salvo after salvo was falling between ten and thirty yards short, but not a single shell struck ; two torpedoes were also fired at us, being well directed, but short. The cruiser was badly damaged by *Arethusa's* 6-inch guns and a splendidly directed fire from *Fearless*, and she shortly afterwards turned away in the direction of Heligoland."

A few minutes after this another German cruiser was sighted, which proved to be the *Mainz*, which was at once engaged by the *Arethusa* and the *Fearless*. A hot fight ensued, for the enemy ship put up a great resistance, but the British shooting was too accurate for her and at the end of about twenty minutes she was on fire and soon after began to settle down by the head, her engines having stopped for some time. She still continued firing, however, but at this moment the Light Cruiser Squadron came on to the scene, and their guns soon reduced the *Mainz* to a mass of wreckage.

At this point of the action one of the most gallant acts of the war was performed, for Admiral Keyes in the *Lurcher*, which had also come up, took his ship alongside the sinking *Mainz*, in spite of the fact that she was on fire and in imminent danger of blowing up, and rescued 220 enemy survivors. Such an act of chivalry, in which the highest pluck and skill were necessary for success, is all the more conspicuous after the action of the German cruiser in firing on the British boats engaged in rescuing Germans from the water earlier in the fight.

An interesting sidelight, and one from quite a novel view-point, is thrown on this action in the following extract from the diary of Lieut. G. F. Bowen, R.N.V.R., who was present on board the *Princess Royal* as an A. B. seaman gunner R.N.V.R. " I arrived down in ' A ' magazine," he writes, " within a few seconds of the ' action ' bugle, and we loaded the hopper and got about five rounds ready in the handing room. Then there was a lull, during which we stripped off to our flannels, opened up plenty of cases and waited. We had not long to wait. ' Bang ' went our right gun, and with a rattling clatter down came the carriage for another round. ' Bang ' went our left gun, and a terrible din followed, which I then took to be our funnels and masts clattering down on to the deck, but which I found later was caused by the descending gun cage of the left gun, and the cage and rammer of the right gun. 'Bang, Bang' off went both guns almost simultaneously, the shaft trembled, and a rush of air swept through the handing room.

"For the next ten minutes they kept us going as hard as we could go. Everyone was merry, and we were singing 'See them shuffle along,' which was most inappropriate; we were singing, I know, because I felt my mouth moving, but what with the discharge of the guns, the clang of the hoists, cages and rammers, and the medley of voices shouting up and down various voice pipes, which, by the way, sounded very hollow and uncanny, we could not hear a word we were singing. We had not the slightest idea of the number of ships we were fighting, what they were, or how our own ship was getting on; we might have been sinking for all we knew. From time to time the men in the gun-house shouted down scraps of news, such as "First ship afire amid-ships—second ship sinking—etc." but this did not convey much. Our surgeon came down and told us that we were badly holed in six places, but as far as we could feel there was no list, so we forgot about it till things should begin to fall sideways.

" At the end of about ten minutes of this rushing about there was a lull, presumably when we had finished off the first of the enemy ships. Off we went again, and the pace kept hot for about fifteen minutes. Then the order ' Cease Fire ' came down, and we knew that we had whacked 'em, whatever they were. We stood easy for a short time, and then the order came down to pack up, and we returned all un-fired charges and went up to see the damage.

" It was disappointing ; one shell only having hit us ; this had entered on the starboard side, presumably a parting shot from the cruiser that first passed us in a sinking condition. It burst in the engine room of the picket boat, completely wrecking it. The ship's plumber, who was in the blacksmith's shop, gave me the following account of the battle. ' It was very misty, and at first I could see nothing but the flashes of their guns, and then out of the mist came one of the enemy cruisers in a sinking condition. We left her on our starboard side ; she fired a parting shot at us as we passed. Then shots began to fall on our port side, a good deal short

THE BELL BUOY

British Submarine and Destroyer entering harbour.

at first, but gradually nearer, till some fell between ourselves and the *Queen Mary*. Two cruisers then emerged from the mist, and we engaged the first; our first shots passed her forward turret clean over the side. The second and third passed one of her funnels over the side. After this two or three struck her under the bridge, and she commenced burning fiercely amidships, and then began to settle down. We then turned our attention to the second, and fired several rounds at her, scoring six or eight hits along her sides from forward to amidships. We lost her in the mist, but I believe she sank eventually."

The *Arethusa* was a perfect glutton for fighting in this action, for as soon as the *Mainz* was dispatched to the bottom Commodore Tyrwhitt searched round for fresh foes to engage, and was soon exchanging shots with the *Köln*, but the range was too great for any effect. It was in this long-range fighting that Admiral Beatty found him when he arrived with the Battle Cruisers, and at once steered to cut off the enemy's retreat to Heligoland, opening fire at full speed. While engaged in this chase another German cruiser appeared ahead out of the mist, and the *Lion* at once broke off the chase to engage this tangible foe. The enemy ship altered course, but was too late to escape punishment. The *Lion* had time to fire two salvos only, but these took effect, and the German cruiser was seen to be burning furiously in a sinking condition before she managed to make her way into a bank of fog. This ship afterwards proved to be the *Ariadne*, and subsequently sank; which fact was admitted by the Germans.

This enemy disposed of, Admiral Beatty continued in pursuit of the *Köln* once more, and after half an hour came up with her. She was badly damaged, but refused to surrender, so fire was opened upon her once more. It was soon all over, a couple of well-directed salvos, and she was sunk.

No more enemy ships being seen, and the increasing number of floating mines that began to be sighted, decided the British Admiral to withdraw his forces; the mists that encircled the Island of Heligoland rendered it inadvisable to carry the pursuit further. Success had crowned the efforts of the attacks; three German cruisers and two destroyers were sunk beyond doubt, and several others so badly damaged that their fate was uncertain; the mists kept their secret that day. Of the British ships not one was sunk, and all returned to their bases, even the *Arethusa* and the *Laurel*, in spite of their wounds.

It was a bold and daring stroke, this carrying of battle into enemy waters, for despite the fog Heligoland was visible to the attackers during part of the action, which was all fought amidst mines and enemy submarines.

The God of Battle was with the British arms this day.

CHAPTER IV.

CORONEL AND THE FALKLAND ISLANDS.

THE action off Coronel in November, 1914, was a preface to the bigger fight off the Falkland Islands some six weeks later. In the former engagement the odds were very much on the foe, for the German Admiral, von Spee, had under his command the armoured cruisers *Scharnhorst* and *Gneisenau,* two of the crack ships of the German navy, and also the light cruisers *Dresden, Leipzig* and *Nürnberg,* while Admiral Sir Christopher Cradock, flying his flag on the cruiser *Good Hope,* had only two other cruisers with him, the *Glasgow* and the *Monmouth,* for the old battleship *Canopus,* though attached to his squadron, was unable to join in the fight, owing to her slow speed in reaching the scene of the fight, and the *Otranto,* an armed liner, was useless against such powerful adversaries, and was ordered to stand clear.

The *Glasgow* was the first to sight enemy;

she was proceeding with the *Monmouth* to support Admiral Cradock in the *Good Hope*, which was a few miles away, when she saw two strange ships on the horizon, which proved to be the *Scharnhorst* and the *Gneisenau*, while some way behind were the *Leipzig* and the *Dresden*. The *Nürnberg* had not yet reached the scene, but she was hurrying up in response to an urgent wireless message from the German Admiral.

On the two British Cruisers joining him, Admiral Cradock, in the *Good Hope*, manœuvred his small force into battle formation. This was about half past five in the afternoon, and the light was already beginning to fail. There was a strong wind, and a big sea was running, certainly not ideal conditions under which to begin a naval action. As the sun went down behind the British ships it made them black masses on the horizon and splendid targets for the enemy gunners, who were the first to open fire. This was replied to at once by our ships, but they were outranged and outgunned by the more modern vessels of the Germans. The *Good Hope* was hit several times by the *Scharnhorst*, while the *Monmouth* was also severely punished by the guns of the *Gneisenau*. The *Leipzig* and the

Dresden were both engaging the *Glasgow*, which was the fastest and probably the most efficient of our ships, but which was no match against two such powerful adversaries, though she put up a very gallant fight.

The fight went on till about eight o'clock, but it was a contest that could have only one end, and when the *Good Hope* caught fire it was but the beginning of this end, as far as that ship was concerned, for soon after this a terrific explosion took place, and before long she went down, the gallant Admiral, who had fought this losing fight so finely, perishing with his ship.

The *Monmouth* was in little better plight, her guns had been silenced and she was on fire, but even then she might have escaped but for an evil chance that led her into the path of the oncoming *Nürnberg*, which was hurrying up to join the action. The result was inevitable, the German cruiser with all her guns intact found an easy prey, and before long the *Monmouth* had gone down to join the flagship. The *Glasgow* with her greater speed and fewer injuries was able to withdraw in safety.

This temporary triumph for the enemy was

but short-lived, and fate, relentless and terrible, had marked them down for destruction. On December 8th, but six weeks after the action off Coronel, von Spee approached the isolated Falkland Islands with a view to capturing them, deeming them easy prey. But on this morning the enemy had the shock of his life, but before we describe the action that followed it will be necessary to trace briefly the facts that led up to this point.

After the Coronel affair the *Glasgow* and the *Canopus* had put into Port Stanley, the only harbour and town in the Islands, where they were later joined, all unknown to the enemy, by a squadron under Vice-Admiral Sturdee, which consisted of the battle cruisers *Invincible* (flying the Admiral's flag) and *Inflexible* and the light cruisers *Carnarvon*, *Cornwall*, *Kent*, and *Bristol*, with the armed merchant ship *Macedonia*.

The *Canopus* was run aground in the inner harbour, where she would be hidden from an approaching force and be able to bring her big guns into play before her presence was revealed, while some of her smaller guns were taken ashore to make land batteries on the hills overlooking the harbour. All the other ships also kept in the outer harbour hidden from the sea, with the exception of the *Macedonia,* who was anchored at the mouth of the harbour as a look-out ship. Watch parties of islanders were stationed on the hill tops, and it was one of these that first reported the approach of the enemy squadron.

It was a peaceful scene that met the eyes of von Spee's men that morning; the weather was calm and visibility good, and they could see the Islands in the distance, with nothing but a merchant ship at anchor outside the harbour. It looked a " soft job " to capture them, but appearances are deceptive, as the Huns soon found to their cost. They approached with their guns trained on the wireless station; if they destroyed the Island's voice she could not call for help, they imagined, little dreaming of the help that was already lying hidden, but waiting for the signal to attack.

It was soon after nine that the *Canopus* opened fire at long range, firing over the spit of land behind which she was hidden. The German ships at once altered course, and made as if to close the *Kent,* which was now outside the harbour, the enemy being still in ignorance of the presence of our two battle-cruisers and the other ships inside.

Then the Germans had their great shock, for as they approached the British squadron put out of harbour and formed up in attack formation. The enemy at once turned tail and made off as fast as he could; it was clearly his object to avoid a fight if possible. Admiral Sturdee, however, thought otherwise, and being master of the situation was able to dictate his terms upon the enemy. The odds were in our favour; we had faster and better gunned ships, the day was young, there was no need for haste, visibility was good and the sea calm.

Accordingly a signal for a general chase was made, and the "fun" began. For a time the enemy, having a good start, maintained their distance, but gradually our ships began to over-haul the flying squadron, and the *Inflexible* opened fire, to be followed in this a few minutes later by the *Invincible*.

The action finally developed into three separate encounters, and we must follow these independently, for this battle was fought over a wide range of sea, in which the various units engaged were not only out of sight of each other at times, but even out of hearing of each other's guns. The first fight was between the battle cruisers *Invincible* and *Inflexible* and the *Carnarvon* against the German armoured cruisers *Scharnhorst* and *Gneisenau*. Finding that they could obtain no safety in flight the two enemy ships were forced to fight, and altered course slightly to bring their guns to bear better on their pursuers, and both sides began a lively exchange of shots. The *Scharnhorst* certainly put up some fine shooting, and managed to hit the *Invincible* several times before she turned and ran once more ; this manœuvre did not help her, for the superior gun-power of the British ships enabled them to continue to punish both the German ships pretty heavily.

The *Scharnhorst* was the first to go ; she was already on fire, and as shot after shot continued to hit her, it was evident that she was in serious difficulties. All at once a great cloud of smoke went up, and she took a heavy list to port ; she continued to sink until she was lying on her beam ends ; here she rested for nearly ten minutes before she took her final plunge to the bottom. In her perished the German Admiral von Spee. There have been blackguards in the German

BLOOD AND IRON AN AIR-RAID IN THE NORTH
DESTROYERS ENGAGING A ZEPPELIN AT
THE MOUTH OF THE TYNE

Navy, as all the world knows, but it is not fair to class von Spee among them. He fought a clean fight, and went down with his flag still flying.

There now remained the *Gneisenau* to be accounted for. Seeing the fate of her consort she turned to fight for her life. Her resistance was brave but unavailing, for by now the slower *Carnarvon* was in the action, and at once opened fire on the doomed cruiser. The German ship continued firing from time to time, and once she managed to hit the *Invincible*, but soon after this her forward funnel was knocked away, and this was really her quietus, for Admiral Sturdee ordered " Cease Fire," but before this could be hoisted the *Gneisenau* opened with a single gun once more. It was a last effort, however; a few more shots sufficed to finish her, she heeled over very suddenly and sank.

Every effort was made by the British to save life, and the boats of the *Invincible* alone rescued 108 men from the water, though owing to the low temperature of the sea many of these were found to be dead when brought aboard.

Thus the two most powerful of the German ships were disposed of, though not without a certain amount of damage. The *Invincible* had suffered most, in fact Admiral Sturdee himself had escaped very narrowly from destruction : he was up in the director-tower on the foremast when one of the tripod legs was shot away.

The second action fought on this day was that between the light cruisers. The *Glasgow*, already war scarred, was swifter than the *Kent* and the *Cornwall*, and soon drew ahead in the chase of the three German ships, the *Leipzig*, *Nürnberg* and *Dresden*. The *Leipzig* was the first of the enemy to be engaged by the *Glasgow*, who held her until the arrival of her slower consorts by means of her superior gunfire. The *Leipzig*, though she put up a good fight, had no chance against the three British ships (for the other German vessels continued to make off as fast as possible), who poured shell after shell into her. Leaving the *Glasgow* and the *Cornwall* to finish off the already doomed *Leipzig*, which finally sank after catching on fire fore and aft, the *Kent* continued her chase of the *Nürnberg*, and the action between these two ships was the third fought on this memorable day.

The chase was a long and stern one, and is historic in the annals of stoking. The *Kent* had not too much coal in her bunkers, but her commander, Captain Allen, determined to catch the German at all costs. Every combustible article was therefore commandeered for the furnaces, tables, chairs, wooden fittings from the officers' cabins, ladders and even deck planking was broken or sawn up to feed the fires. Her full speed was 22 knots, but this day she did over 25.

Gradually the *Kent* drew nearer the enemy till she was able to open fire, a fire returned at once by the *Nürnberg*. The *Kent's* gunners were finding their mark again and again, and the German ship was also hitting the British one, pretty severely at times, but nothing like so often as she was being punished herself. For about an hour this running fight was kept up, but the enemy was gradually weakening till the *Nurnberg* caught fire, soon after which her gunfire ceased. The *Kent* drew closer, and began pounding away at her again, for her flag was still flying, but in a minute or two it was hauled down and she surrendered. It was too late, however, for she was now little more than a blazing wreck, with a heavy list to starboard. The end was not far off, for while the *Kent* was patching up her damaged boats to save life if possible, the German vessel disappeared with a hiss that could be heard for miles.

Only twelve men of the *Nürnberg's* crew were able to be rescued, and seven of these eventually died. It was one of the most thrilling single ship actions of the whole war, and the fact that victory was ours is undoubtedly due to the *Kent's* engineers.

A final and small action took place off Falkland Islands while the larger battle was in progress. At the commencement of the chase three enemy ships were seen approaching from the opposite direction, and the *Bristol* and the *Macedonia* were ordered, to investigate and engage. These proved to be German transports, which probably were making for the Islands with the intention of forcing a landing. One of these managed to escape, but the other two, the *Santa Isabel* and the *Baden* were sunk by the *Bristol* after capture and removal of the crews.

This ended one of the completest victories on the naval front; four German ships were sunk, the *Dresden* alone escaping in the darkness (to be sunk a few months afterwards off Juan Fernandez). We lost no ships, and our total

AN INCIPIENT MINEFIELD

casualties in killed and wounded were under thirty. This victory put an end to all German hopes of commerce raiding, for the few enemy ships that were still at large were already marked down for destruction and in about six months after this not a German ship remained afloat in these seas.

CHAPTER V.

THE BATTLE OF DOGGER BANK.

THE action off the Dogger Bank on January 24th, 1915, was an accident as far as the German ships were concerned. Their object in leaving port was not to give battle but to make a dash for some part of the English Coast, do as much damage as they could to an undefended town, and then make home with all speed ; a plan which the enemy had recently carried out at Great Yarmouth, Scarborough and Hartlepool.

In the present case, however, he had reckoned without his host, and when that host proves to be a strong force of Battle Cruisers under Sir David Beatty it is an unpleasant factor to be considered by the enemy. It was soon after seven in the morning that the British Admiral first had news of enemy ships in the vicinity, when the sound and flash of guns was heard and observed to the south-east, and a signal from the cruiser *Aurora* soon reached the flagship that she was in contact with the enemy. The *Aurora* had been patrolling ahead of the main fleet, and just as it began to get light she had sighted a four-funnelled ship on the horizon about four miles away. The *Aurora* at once closed to ascertain who she might be, reserving her fire for a time, as in the half-light of morning it was hard to tell if she were a friend or a foe. All doubt on this point was soon settled, for as the *Aurora* approached, the stranger, which was accompanied by several destroyers, opened fire. The British cruiser at once replied, and soon found the range, when she poured shell after shell at the *Kolberg*—for such the German cruiser proved to be—so that the latter soon gave up the fight and fell back upon the stronger force which the increasing light now showed up.

Meanwhile Admiral Beatty had increased speed and was rushing up to intercept the enemy squadron, which was found to consist of the *Blücher, Derfflinger, Seydlitz,* and *Moltke,* with six light cruisers and a number of destroyers.

Admiral Beatty had under him in this action the *Lion* (his flagship), *Princess Royal, Tiger, New Zealand* and *Indomitable,* with four light cruisers —the *Southampton, Nottingham, Birmingham,* and

Lowestoft, while the *Arethusa*, under Commodore Tyrwhitt, the *Aurora* and *Undaunted*, with destroyer flotillas from Harwich, were supporting him.

As soon as our main forces began to appear the German ships altered course, and it became obvious that they had no wish to engage if it could be avoided, and if a fight took place at all it would be a running one. The morning was clear, with good visibility, and the British squadrons settled down to a long and stern chase, and gradually began to overhaul the flying enemy, in spite of the latter's frantic efforts to reach the shelter of their own minefields before our ships got near enough to engage.

The *Lion* was the first to open fire, but her shots fell short, and for a time she had to content herself with single shots to test the range as she gradually drew nearer, and about nine o'clock, after an hour and a half's hard chase, she made her first hit on the *Blücher*, which was fourth in the German line, with the *Derfflinger*, *Moltke* and *Seydlitz* ahead. Once having found the range the *Lion's* shooting was very accurate, and several more shots were seen to take effect on the *Blücher*. On the *Princess Royal* coming into range she at once opened fire on the *Blücher*, while the *Lion* transferred her attentions to the *Seydlitz*, which was just ahead of the larger German ship.

At first the enemy did not respond, but when they realised that escape from their pursuers was hopeless they began to return our fire, without inflicting much damage to our ships at first. The *New Zealand* had now joined the fight, also opening on the *Blücher*, while the *Princess Royal* took the *Seydlitz* for her target. The shooting of the *Princess Royal* was most accurate, and hit after hit was recorded upon the enemy ship, which was soon ablaze, while the *Tiger* was doing equally good work upon the *Derfflinger*, the leading ship in the German line, which was also under the fire of the *Lion*.

The enemy destroyers now began to emit vast clouds of smoke with the intention of screening their larger ships, and behind this the enemy altered course. Their battle cruisers were in a bad way, the *Blücher*, hit again and again, was seen to be lagging behind and on fire; while another fire had also broken out on the *Derfflinger*, as well as the one already mentioned on the *Seydlitz*, which had suffered so severely from the guns of the *Princess Royal*.

The *Blücher* fell farther and farther astern of her consorts, who had apparently abandoned her to her fate, and the main action had now swept on past her. The crippled *Blücher* turned northwards and tried to drag herself, like some wounded animal, out of immediate danger. She had a heavy list as well as the fire which was raging fiercely still, one funnel was gone and the other two tottering, her foremast had been shot away and part of her mainmast, while her forward turret had been carried over the side.

The *Indomitable* was told off to stand by and finish the enemy ship, which reeled from each successive broadside. The *Arethusa* put two torpedoes into her, and the final stroke was given by the destroyer *Meteor*, who discharged a torpedo into her at close range. There was a violent explosion, and the *Blücher* turned over on her side and began to settle down. Men leaped up on to her side and plunged into the water, and in a few minutes the huge German ship had disappeared for ever beneath the water.

The diary of Lieut. G. F. Bowen, R.N.V.R., who was on the *Princess Royal*, contains some notes about this engagement that are worth quoting as a personal record : " At 7 a.m. " he says,

" we went to action stations steaming along at about 20 knots, with four light cruisers on our port beam and about twenty destroyers spread out well ahead so that they looked just black dots on the horizon. At 8.15 a.m. Mr. Langdale came out of X Turret, and informed us that German Battle Cruisers had been sighted by our light cruisers. At about 8.25 several bright flashes showed on the horizon on our port bow. Our destroyers and light cruisers immediately commenced to belch forth thick columns of black smoke, and a large bow wave appeared and a long white wash behind them, indicating that there was something doing.

" We increased speed till we were doing about 28 knots. *Indomitable* and *New Zealand* following us looked grand as they cleaved their way through the water, from time to time taking clouds of spray over their fo'castles. The morning was dull and gray, and seemed to make them look even more sinister and formidable. On our starboard bow the *Lion* and *Tiger* were forging along; the *Tiger*, as is her custom, ploughing straight through everything, so that her bows were always covered with spray, while a constant waterfall ran down her sides. Clouds of smoke on the horizon, showing where the enemy were, were very gradually drawing nearer, and at about 8.45 decks were cleared for action. The first shot was soon afterwards fired. We opened at about 22,000 yards, going down to 20,000. After the first few shots we commenced salvos, and the fun was fast and furious. All we could hear below, however, was the banging of the guns, and could get no news of how the battle was going. From time to time messages were sent down saying that first one side of the ship was dangerous and then the other, and we expected a projectile to come through every minute. Twice the 4-inch gun's crews were called up and twice sent down again. Then came the order ' stand by the aerial gun's crew.' Then we were all shifted to the port side, where we waited in the semi-darkness of the oil lamps, the electric light having been switched off, listening to the banging of our guns and getting covered with dirt which came from goodness knows where. As usual rumours came down about the rate of one per minute.

" Then an airship was sighted. ' Prepare for aerial attack ' was sounded, and we manned our gun. The Zep., however, kept well out of range, so we did not get a shot at her, but turned our attention instead to the sinking *Blücher*. She was heavily afire amidships and gradually heeling over, and through the telescope of the gun I could see men running about in great confusion on the decks. The last we saw of her was when she was lying on her side and our destroyers were hurrying up to the rescue.

" We then carried on with the chase of the flying Huns. Owing to the damage to the *Lion's* engines she was compelled to draw out of the line, and Admiral Beatty came alongside us in the destroyer *Attack* and clambered aboard with great agility over the torpedo net shelf. Great cheers went up. The action was broken off, and we turned back at about five bells, over-hauling the *Lion*. She had a list to port, and was holed in about seven places of her port side, but was getting along under her own steam. We made preparations to tow her, but it was found to be unnecessary, and we went ahead, leaving the destroyers to escort her."

The *Meteor*, which was commanded by Lieut. F. T. Peters, was badly damaged in this action in a fight with the enemy destroyers, which our " M " Division, under Capt. The Hon. H. Meade, had frustrated in their attempted torpedo attack on the *Lion* and the *Tiger*, and consequently she was not in a condition to do much rescue work, but the *Arethusa* remained behind and picked up many of the survivors from the *Blucher* who were struggling in the water. While engaged in this humane work a Zeppelin and a German sea-plane appeared on the scene and dropped bombs on rescuers and rescued alike, an act which no one but a German would ever contemplate.

Meanwhile the main action had been continued, and the British squadron was still in pursuit of the enemy.

The *Lion* had been hit repeatedly, for it was the main target of all the German ships, and the *Tiger* had also received some punishment. It was soon found that though the wounds of the *Lion* were not vital they would reduce her speed considerably, so Admiral Beatty boarded the destroyer *Attack*, and carried on at full speed to overtake the other battle cruisers, who had now outdistanced him.

The enemy, however, had by this time begun to reach home waters, and the dangers of mines and submarine attacks rendered it inadvisable to carry the pursuit any farther, and about noon Admiral Beatty met his other ships returning, and subsequently transferred his flag to the *Princess Royal*.

This ended the battle of the Dogger Bank, and it was nothing but bad luck on our part that allowed the enemy to gain the shelter of his own mine fields, after running away the whole fight as fast as his engines could take him, for had the *Lion* not been disabled by a chance shot at the most critical point of the pursuit, there is no doubt that the already severely damaged *Derfflinger* and *Seydlitz* would have been caught and sunk; but the victory, unfortunately not so complete as might have been, at least taught the Germans that they could not dash out and raid our coast with impunity, and that the North Sea was still, as it always has been and always will be, the free cruising ground for our Navy.

All our ships got back to port safely, though the *Lion*, the *Tiger* and the *Meteor* bore the honourable scars of war more plainly than the rest, several of whom were hit, but not badly. Of all the damage the most serious was that on board the *Lion*, which had to be taken in tow by the *Indomitable*, a difficult task, owing to

the condition of the former ship and the state
of the sea, and one which caused much anxiety
at the time, but by skilful handling the wounded
Lion was got home safely, and was soon repaired
and ready for the sea again, as the Germans
found to their cost about a year later when she
showed her teeth once more at the Battle of
Jutland.

"SHIPPING IT GREEN"

Super-Dreadnought driving into a heavy sea.

CHAPTER VI.

THE BATTLE OF JUTLAND.

IT is not my intention in this chapter to take any side or part in the controversy regarding the Battle of Jutland, but merely to tell the story of the action, and the main incidents in it, as they actually occurred.

On May 31st, 1916, the Grand Fleet, under Admiral Jellicoe, had left its Base at Scapa Flow for one of its periodical sweeps of the North Sea. On many previous occasions on which this had been done no sign of German ships had been seen, but on this memorable day an event took place that had long been hoped for in the British Fleet — the enemy was sighted on the horizon.

The first ship to make a report to this effect was the light cruiser *Galatea*, under Commodore E. S. Alexander-Sinclair, who, at about 2.30 that afternoon, sighted two enemy cruisers to the eastward, and soon after saw the smoke of a much larger force towards the north-east. A sea-plane from the *Engadine* was sent up to reconnoitre, which closed the enemy, and flying low was able to observe his disposition. It is interesting to note that this was the first occasion of the use of a sea-plane in actual warfare, and the excellent results obtained showed how valuable this new arm of the Service was likely to prove; which opinion has been so fully justified subsequently. The sea-plane came under very heavy fire from the enemy ships, but owing to skilful piloting by Lieut. F. J. Rutland, returned safely with information as to the strength and disposition of the enemy ships.

The Battle Cruisers, under Sir David Beatty, at once opened fire at a range of about 23,000 yards, rapidly closing the enemy the while till they were within 18,000 yards of the German Fleet. The firing of the latter at this juncture was very accurate, and before long the *Lion*, Admiral Beatty's flagship, was hit twice, and the *Tiger* and the *Princess Royal* also suffered damage. Our fire was also effective, and several hits were seen to be made. Still the two fleets closed, and at 16,000 yards the fire was very fierce on both sides. The *Indefatigable* was soon in serious trouble, and was seen sinking by the stern, the result of an explosion in her magazine. She fell out of line, but was again hit as she did so, and before long she began to settle down very rapidly, finally turning turtle and sinking. This was the first British ship to be sunk in the action.

Meanwhile our destroyers were waiting a favourable moment to attack, and their chance soon came when a light cruiser and fifteen destroyers were seen to detach themselves from the enemy fleet. Twelve of our destroyers, headed by the *Nestor*, under Commander the Hon. E. B. S. Bingham, at once gave chase to engage them before they could carry out their projected plans, whatever they might be. A fierce fight took place at close range, with the result that the enemy manœuvre was frustrated. The losses were equal on both sides; we sank two of the enemy's ships, but the *Nestor* and the *Nomad* were so badly damaged that they could not rejoin the British forces, and were subsequently sunk by the main German Fleet when it came up.

In the meantime the Battle Squadron had come up and was in action, but at very long range. The *Barham* was soon hit, but carried on with the fight, but the *Queen Mary* was not so fortunate, for the same fate befell her that had overtaken the *Indefatigable*, a magazine blew up; a huge cloud of smoke hid her from view, and when it cleared away all trace of the ship had vanished; she must have sunk almost immediately after the explosion.

The Main Battle Fleet now turned northwards to manœuvre for a better position, but the fight was gallantly continued by the Battle Cruisers. The Germans had also suffered, and three of their largest ships had been seen to sink, besides several of their destroyers. Visibility began to get very bad, especially towards the enemy, who also made use of smoke screens, behind which he manœuvred his ships into new positions.

It was at this period of the action that the *Chester*, under Captain R. N. Lawson, put up her very gallant fight against three German ships, in the course of which the boy V.C., the brave little Jack Cornwall, was killed. How this lad, who was only 16 years old, remained at his post by the gun when all the rest of the gun's crew had been killed, was one of the most noble actions of the war, and is too well known for any need to repeat the story in detail. The *Chester*, though badly damaged, managed to regain her flotilla, though not before she had inflicted severe punishment upon the vastly superior (in point of numbers, but in nothing else) force opposed to her.

The destroyers were again busy, especially the *Shark*, the *Acasta*, the *Ophelia* and the *Christopher*, which attacked a squadron of German cruisers. In this encounter the *Shark* was sunk, but fighting fiercely to the end. Commander Loftus Jones refused to surrender but continued to direct and cheer his men till the very last, even though he had lost a leg in the early part of the engagement.

The survivors fought till the last gun was put out of action, and a few seconds after the ship was hit by a torpedo, and went down with the White Ensign still flying. The very gallant commander was drowned, and only six men from the whole of the ship's company were picked up, and even then not until the next morning.

The *Defence* and the *Warrior* were now engaged with four enemy cruisers, and once more the deadly magazine explosions were the undoing of one of our ships, for after sinking a German cruiser, a shell struck the *Defence*, which was fatal from this cause, and she sank. The *Warrior*, though badly damaged, continued the fight until she managed to get clear. The *Warspite*, which was coming to her help, came in for some punishment owing to her helm jamming at a critical time, and the *Duke of Edinburgh* also joined in the engagement with the *Black Prince*. There is still some mystery as to the fate of the latter, for she disappeared completely; probably she passed on beyond the zone of the immediate action and came upon another German squadron, where she met her end fighting against vastly overwhelming odds, or possibly she may have been torpedoed by a German submarine, which was known to be somewhere about the vicinity.

The *Lion* was constantly in action, and Admiral Beatty led the Battle Cruiser Squadron in a masterly manner against much heavier forces, and had it not been for his wonderful handling of his flotilla our losses must certainly have been greater. In this action the Germans used special long-range torpedoes, and a very high skill in manœuvring was shown by both the Battle Cruisers and the Battle Fleet in escaping these.

The main Battle Fleet now began to come into action in earnest, and it was about this time that the *Invincible* (Rear Admiral the Hon.

Horace Hood) went down, when she was engaged
in company with the *Lion*, the *Indomitable*, and
the *Inflexible* in an encounter with enemy battle
cruisers. Still again it was a magazine explosion
that was the cause; this time it broke the ship
completely in two, and only five of her crew
were saved by a destroyer. She was seen after
with her bow and her stern both sticking out
of the water in a most curious way, and it is
thought that she must have been over a sand-
bank at the time.

Very gallant work was accomplished by the
destroyer *Onslow*, which, by sinking a German
destroyer undoubtedly saved a torpedo attack
upon the *Lion*; Lieut.-Commander Tovey, who
was in command, then continued on and attacked
a battle cruiser, and after that fired the rest of
his torpedoes at the German battleships. The
Onslow was severely damaged, and would have
been sunk had not Lieut.-Commander Palmer
in the destroyer *Defender*, although his own ship
was also damaged, come to her rescue under
very heavy fire and towed her back to safety.

The visibility was getting worse and worse,
and a sea-fog that was getting thicker every
hour greatly impeded the work of the Battle

Fleet, but nevertheless the shooting was still accurate and telling, for about this time two German battle cruisers were seen to be on fire and another was observed to explode and sink rapidly. Our own Battle Cruisers were hotly engaged ahead, and the destroyers were still doing splendid work, both supported by the guns of the Battle Fleet. The *Iron Duke* (flying Admiral Jellicoe's flag) now had a sharp encounter with an enemy battleship, which she hit with her second salvo and poured shells into her till the German ship gave up the fight and retired. Night was fast approaching, and the Germans managed to get away in a damaged condition, and it became obvious now that the Battle Fleet was doing such effective work that the enemy tactics were to avoid further action as much as possible, and in this they were aided by the bad visibility.

It was necessary, as evening wore on, to think about the disposition of the Fleet for the night, and to guard as far as was possible against torpedo attacks from destroyers in the hours of darkness, and to be in a favourable position for renewing the fight at dawn.

During the night that followed the larger

FIGHTING THE LAST GUN

Gallant end of H.M.S. *Tipperary* at Jutland.

of the British ships were not attacked, owing to the skill with which they were placed, and our destroyers were very active in delivering many daring and successful attacks on the enemy and inflicting heavy loss upon him. How much damage was done to his ships is very hard to estimate under the circumstances, for night fighting of this sort is always uncertain, when in the darkness and smoke it is often easy to mistake friend for foe.

In one of these attacks the destroyer *Tipperary* was sunk, but not before she succeeded in sinking a German light cruiser, and the *Spitfire* collided with another enemy cruiser and damaged her so considerably that she was forced to retire from the action. A German battleship (thought to be the *Pommern*, but in the darkness there was some doubt) was sunk by three of our destroyers, the *Ardent,* the *Ambuscade,* and the *Garland,* while shortly afterwards two more enemy ships were seen to explode. The *Maenad* was responsible for yet another, while the *Faulknor* led a wonderful dash against six large enemy ships and sank one of them.

It was a night of horror for the enemy and of the fiercest fighting on both sides ; our destroyers seemed to come out of the darkness to strike their vital blows and to disappear again almost at once. Searchlights flashed on and off, for to keep on one too long was to court attack, and the great white splashes, like ghostly pillars, seemed to be perpetual on every side, so great was the firing.

All at once a large enemy vessel was seen to cross the destroyer lines, firing heavily as she went; she was going at high speed, and in her course she rammed the *Turbulent* and sank her and damaged the *Petard* by her gun-fire. The *Castor* sank an enemy destroyer soon after this, engaging her at point blank range, while the *Moresby* attacked four battleships and sank one. All along the line our destroyers were very fiercely engaged, and how much damage they managed to inflict upon the enemy will perhaps never be known; certainly it was more than the Germans ever admitted, but it is known that at least five German battleships and a cruiser were hit by torpedoes, though in every case there was not time for them to sink before the attackers had withdrawn. Again, there were times when it was hard to tell which of a particular flotilla of destroyers was actually responsible for the damage, as in many cases they fired their torpedoes simultaneously, and in addition to this our movements were very badly hampered by fog. There is no doubt that these night attacks by the destroyers put a finishing touch to the battle, and were instrumental in the withdrawal of the enemy fleet.

Two of our light cruisers, the *Southampton* and the *Dublin*, were in action during the night with five enemy cruisers; the fight was short but fierce, and after about fifteen minutes the enemy withdrew; it is thought that one German cruiser was sunk in this engagement; she was seen to be in great difficulties. Both the *Southampton* and the *Dublin* suffered rather heavy casualties, especially the former, where fire broke out, but was luckily got under before it reached the magazine.

During all this fierce and exciting fighting one British ship had " slunk away " ! She was a small ship, and had managed to get off unobserved by the enemy, and her " slinking " off was the means of several enemy vessels being lost. This gallant little ship was the mine-layer *Abdiel*, who managed to work her way to the homeward track that the enemy would have to make when he left the scene of the battle to return to his base. Here the *Abdiel* laid a special minefield, and Captain Curtis, who was in command, did his work well, for from reports of a submarine on patrol near Horn Reef several violent underwater explosions were heard, which from their position could only have come from the German Fleet hurrying home, and another ship reported having received quite a number of S.O.S. wireless messages at this time. It would be interesting to learn how many enemy ships were sunk in this way; it was a secret they never divulged, and of course it was impossible for us to count them among their losses owing to the uncertainty of it, but there is no doubt among naval men that this last blow was a very effective one, and resulted in a serious loss to the enemy fleet.

When dawn broke the fog was very thick, and no sign of the German Fleet could be seen by our main forces, though a Zeppelin was sighted, but which made off upon heavy high-angle fire being directed upon it, and the destroyer *Sparrowhawk*, which was lying in a very badly damaged condition to the eastward of the fleet, sighted a German cruiser steaming towards them. The *Sparrowhawk* expected an attack, and prepared

WINGS OF THE FLEET

Cruiser and Seaplanes on patrol.

to defend herself as best she could, but, to the astonishment of those on board the destroyer, as the enemy ship got within range she did not open fire and appeared to be slowing up, and then, with startling suddenness, she commenced to sink by the bows and subsequently disappeared. The *Sparrowhawk* was later on picked up by four of our destroyers, but was too badly holed to tow, so after her crew had been transferred she was sunk.

The Germans certainly showed wonderful cleverness in manœuvring during their retirement in the darkness, but had it not been for the thick fog, which formed so effective a screen over all their doings, they would certainly never have got away without a running fight. The Grand Fleet cruised about and searched the vicinity till noon, but not a sign of the enemy could be seen, so it returned, though with reluctance, to Scapa Flow and Rosyth. Unfortunately the *Warrior*, which had to be taken in tow by the sea-plane ship *Engadine*, had to be abandoned, as weather conditions made it impossible to tow her further in her damaged condition. Shortly after her crew had been taken off she sank. Several of the destroyers were so badly damaged that they required assistance, but managed to get back eventually, though some were delayed by the rough sea that was now running.

It may seem from this account, in the mention of our ships being sunk, that we lost more ships than the Germans, but this was not so. Although hard to tell at night, the losses of the enemy were known to be five battleships, five battle cruisers, nine destroyers and four submarines. These figures are, of course, not counting those ships that were lost by the enemy in his retirement as a result of the mines laid by the *Abdiel*.

Our own losses were five cruisers—*Indefatigable, Queen Mary, Defence, Black Prince* and *Warrior*; and the destroyers *Nestor, Nomad, Shark, Tipperary, Ardent, Fortune, Sparrowhawk* and *Turbulent*. This makes the total known losses to be 13 British ships as against 22 German.

Much as the loss of our own fine ships is to be regretted the loss to the personnel of the Fleet was more serious still; some of the finest officers and men went down with their ships, and though the casualty list is too long to quote here it contained such fine sailors as Rear-Admiral Sir Robert Arbuthnot, Rear-Admiral the Hon. Horace Hood, and Captains Sowerby, Prowse Cay,

Bonham, Wintour and Ellis; names already famous in naval annals and more famous still in the annals of England after their gallant death in action.

The subsequent claim of the Germans, that the Battle of Jutland was a victory for them, is taken whence it came, and no one who has studied the matter can give it a serious thought.

It is a significant fact that after returning to its base on June 1st the Grand Fleet at once coaled and reported ready for sea before 10 p.m. on the following day. A beaten fleet does not do that sort of thing, any more than a victorious fleet hastens back to harbour in the darkness to stay there without showing its nose outside for two and a half years, and then only emerge to surrender tamely without striking a blow in its defence!

The Battle of Jutland was the death-knell of German naval power, as far as their High Seas Fleet was concerned.

CHAPTER VII.

THE DOVER PATROL.

Of all the deeds that helped to win the war the work of the Dover Patrol would be found hard to beat for persistence, for gallantry, or for strenuous and dangerous tasks carried out under most nerve-racking conditions.

From the moment of the declaration of war until the signing of the armistice the ships on this patrol kept ceaseless and ever-wakeful vigil, not only on the narrow stretch of water that separates England and France but also on the waters adjacent, up into the North Sea on one side and down into the English Channel on the other. The safety of the British Army was in its keeping.

On the general life on patrol I have already written, and it was just the same in these waters, except that the moments of excitement were more frequent and perhaps the whole work a little more nerve-racking on account of the

ST. GEORGE AND THE DRAGON   ZEPPELIN L15
IN THE THAMES

By the courtesy of the Imperial War Museum

narrow waters—though they seemed wide enough on a night patrol!

In the early part of the war twenty miles of submarine nets were laid parallel to the Belgian coast, and the task of watching these at night was part of the daily routine—as an Irish officer remarked to me once—and later on these were taken up in favour of another net barrage from the Goodwin Sands to the Dyck Light Vessel off the French Coast. These net defences, however, though useful and to a certain extent effective in preventing U-Boats from getting through to the English Channel or returning that way to Zeebrugge from the Irish Sea, had their disadvantages. Owing to the strong currents and rough weather it was found difficult to keep them in proper repair, so towards the end of 1917 the famous Folkstone-Gris-Nez minefield was laid. This differed from other minefields in several particulars, the chief one being that the mines were laid at different depths from about thirty feet below the surface to the bed of the sea. These were very thickly strewn, so that a submarine submerging would have an equal chance of hitting one at whatever depth it went to escape the watching patrol.

At first huge lights known as Dover flares, and each a million candle-power, were lit at frequent intervals every fifteen minutes or so to show up the sea for nearly a mile radius so clearly that a submarine that might be endeavouring to steal through on the surface coming within this arc of light would be forced to dive (as they never fought in these strongly guarded waters if they could avoid it, for there could be but one end to such an encounter) among the thickly laid mines, often never to come to the surface again except in pieces.

The effect of these flares was very weird. I remember the first time I saw one. It had been let off by a trawler to which we were approaching from the dark side, and looked exactly as if she were on fire. A great burst of flame suddenly lit up the blackness of night, everything on the trawler, about half a mile ahead, was brightly and ruddily illuminated at first till the flare was at its height, when the masts and bridge were brilliant white, with the hull in black outline where the deep shadows were cast. Altogether it was a most striking effect.

In the latter days of the war these flares were discontinued, their place being taken by Barrage

Vessels, placed in a line at two-mile intervals from Dover to the French Coast. These ships were fitted with two extremely powerful searchlights, capable of sweeping the surface of the sea for a wide area. These bright lights were feared by the U-Boats even more than the flares on account of their mobility.

This barrage was very successful, as many a German submarine found to its cost, for when they once got within the range of these relentless searching eyes there was no escape for them; to remain on the surface meant that they must be destroyed by the guns of the patrol craft, and if they submerged death was waiting for them in the depths.

To recount in detail all the deeds of the ships that kept these narrow waters would be impossible here, even if such a record could be compiled, which I doubt, for many things happened, in some cases "minor incidents" that find no place in official dispatches, which are nevertheless thrilling stories in themselves. One famous story must suffice now, and no better one could be chosen than the encounter of the *Swift* and the *Broke* with six German destroyers, which may truly be called "An Epic of the Dover Patrol."

The night of April 20-21, 1917, had been an exceptionally dark one, an ideal night for raiders, when two ships could pass within a few hundred yards of each other unnoticed, and it was upon this night that the Germans had chosen to send six of their fastest destroyers from Zeebrugge out to do what damage they could before the daylight which they hated might reveal their presence to their foes. These destroyers managed to send a few shells into Dover and a good many into Calais, and were proceeding back to port at full speed when they had the misfortune, from their point of view, to run into two British destroyers (almost literally owing to the darkness) that were on a mid-channel patrol. These two vessels that this night became famous in British Naval History were the *Swift*, under Commander Ambrose Peck, and the *Broke*, under Commander E. R. Evans, the latter officer already well-known as a Polar explorer under Captain Scott.

The sea was quite calm, but so black was the night that the German ships were almost upon the British before either look-outs could see what was ahead. In a second all was changed, when the *Swift's* look-out man reported the

DESTROYERS MAKING A SMOKE SCREEN

presence of six destroyers ahead. It was certain
at once that they were enemy ships, for none of
our own would be steaming eastwards at such a
rate at this time of night. Almost at the same
moment the Germans spotted the two ships
ahead, and immediately opened fire without
slacking speed.

The captain of the *Swift* was a rapid thinker,
he realised that as the enemy were travelling
at such a speed in the opposite direction they
would soon be out of sight in the darkness and
that gun-fire would be uncertain, so at once
turning at right angles to his course, he made
to ram the leading ship of the six at full speed
and in the teeth of a hot point-blank fire. The
attacker's target was none too big and moving
rapidly, and the *Swift* missed it by a fraction,
only narrowly escaping being rammed herself
by the next in line, but by a superb piece of
seamanship Commander Peck swung his ship
like a flash in time to launch a torpedo at another
in the enemy line, and hit. Then he set off at
full speed in chase of still another.

Here we must leave her for a moment while
we follow the doings of her consort. Attacking
at the same time as the *Swift* the *Broke* was

successful in hitting her mark with her first torpedo as well as pouring round after round of shell into her, and then she, too, prepared to ram. This was the crux of the battle and one of the most dramatic and daring actions in the war. Dashing on at a terrific speed the *Broke* hit the German destroyer almost amidships, nearly splitting her in two. Then began a fight that recalls the days of Nelson and the feats of boarding. So tightly wedged was the *Broke* in the sides of the other ship that at first she could not free herself, but she continued to engage the enemy with every gun still in action, though she herself was undergoing severe punishment from the rest of the German flotilla within range. A crowd of Germans now began to swarm over her fo'castle, and a fierce hand-to-hand fight ensued, in which Midshipman Donald Gyles, R.N.R., who had been in charge of one of the forward guns, with two or three men met the rush and actually held up the invaders till a fresh party, armed with cutlasses, came to the rescue and cleared the decks, capturing some prisoners. The fight was short, but it was full of thrills, and by the time it was over the *Broke* had managed to clear herself of the sinking ship,

H.M.S. *BROKE* RAMMING THE GERMAN DESTROYER.

and set off in pursuit of the flying enemy. Once again she tried to ram, in spite of the damage to her bows, but this time she just missed her prey, but was able to hit another ship with a torpedo.

The Germans by this time had almost given up the fight, and were only firing spasmodically; all their efforts were needed in the mad rush for port that was now engaging their best attention. The *Broke*, though not able to maintain her full speed, managed to draw level with one of the German ships that was on fire. The men on her were shouting wildly for help, and Commander Evans very gallantly proceeded to close her, though at very great risk to his own vessel. As he did so the Germans suddenly opened fire; one of those acts of treachery that had stained the annals of the German navy for all time. This time the enemy was amply repaid for their foul deed. A few rounds from the *Broke*, and a torpedo which hit fairly amidships, sent the ship and its traitorous crew to the bottom.

While all this was going on, the *Swift*, owing to damage to herself, was unable to catch the fleeing German of which she had been in pursuit, and turned back to see if she could render any help to her consort, and on her return came upon the destroyer that had been rammed by the *Broke* in a sinking condition. The sailors on board her were also calling for help, but the *Swift*, fearing treachery, held off for a little keeping her guns trained on the enemy. However, the ship was done for, and presently she heeled over and sank. All sight of other enemy ships having disappeared the *Swift* carried on with the work of rescue, even using her search-lights to aid her.

This brought the *Broke*, who had also lost touch with the enemy, on to the scene, and it was evident that the fight was over. It had been short, dramatically short—a bare five minutes, but it is one that will live. Two of Germany's newest destroyers were sunk, two more so badly damaged that it is quite possible, though they may have managed to escape for the moment, that they never reached port, and over a hundred German officers and men were taken prisoner. I doubt if any five minutes of the war could beat it for fierce action and tangible result.

Many and varied were the tasks allotted to the Dover Patrol. The Downs Boarding Flotilla, which had its headquarters at Ramsgate, and did such fine service, especially in the early years of the war, was under the protection of this patrol, and the task of guarding often over a hundred merchantmen, anchored in the Downs awaiting examination, from the attacks of German submarines, was no small one. Then the " policing " of the Belgian Coast and the keeping of the Huns more or less in that region also lay within the " beat " of the watchers from Dover.

The latter task was an arduous one and led to much fighting, which began in the autumn of 1914, and continued, off and on, until the armistice. The Dover Patrol might almost be termed the left flank of the British Army, for in the first October of the war, during that critical time when the Germans were making a bid for the coast ports as far as Calais, the naval forces under Rear-Admiral the Hon. Horace Hood stemmed the enemy advance and held them up at Nieuport, from which point they never advanced. The Monitors *Mersey*, *Severn* and *Humber*, with the cruisers *Attentive* and *Foresight*, were the chief ships engaged, with later on the old battleship *Venerable*. A flotilla of destroyers also took part, the *Falcon* distinguishing herself in these attacks.

For three weeks these ships kept up a fierce fire on the advancing German hordes, and a party from the *Severn* were landed with machine guns at Nieuport to do splendid work under Lieut. E. S. Wise, who was unluckily killed just at the moment when the oncoming Germans were finally checked.

Of the result of these operations Admiral Hood wrote, "The presence of the ships on the coast soon caused alterations in the enemy's plans, less and less of their troops were seen, while more and more heavy guns were gradually mounted along the sand dunes that fringe the coast. It gradually became apparent that the rush of the enemy along the coast had been checked, that the operations were developing into a trench warfare, and that the work of the flotilla had, for the moment, ceased."

In these coastal attacks a flotilla of French destroyers assisted the British, and it is interesting to note that on one occasion Admiral Hood led the fleet into action on a French ship, flying his flag on the *Intrepide*.

When Vice-Admiral Sir Reginald H. Bacon replaced Rear-Admiral Hood the attacks on the Belgian Coast were renewed by further bombardments, and the story of what was done under his command is perhaps best summarised in his own words in one of his dispatches :

" In the summer and autumn of this year," he wrote in December, 1915, " circumstances enabled offensive operations to be undertaken from the sea at certain points on the Belgian Coast. In all cases great care has been taken to confine the fire of the guns to objectives of military and naval importance so as to inflict the minimum of loss of life and distress on the civil population. In order to carry this principle into effect, it has at times been necessary to modify and even postpone projected attacks. The results, therefore, have been effective rather than sensational."

On the evening of August 22nd the harbour and defences of Zeebrugge were attacked, and of this operation Admiral Bacon says : " The results were markedly successful ; all the objectives selected were damaged or destroyed. It was satisfactory that extreme accuracy was obtained with the gun-fire at the long ranges necessary for the best attack of such defences.

" On September 6th another attack was made and damage done to submarine workshops and harbour works. The enemy returned our fire with heavy guns of calibre probably larger than our own and with considerable accuracy. Again the shooting on the part of our vessels was remarkably good, and the assistance rendered by the Auxiliary Craft most valuable."

The enemy on the coast were given little rest at this time, and before the end of September six other attacks had taken place, and on October 2nd another big bombardment was carried out, of which the Admiral says: " The whole coast during our passage was showing signs of considerable alarm and unrest as a result of the previous operations. Our advanced vessels were attacked by submarines, but without success."

Six more attacks were undertaken before the end of November: " The damage inflicted on the enemy is known to include the sinking of one torpedo boat, two submarines and one large dredger, the total destruction of three military factories and damage to a fourth, expensive damage to the locks at Zeebrugge and the destruction of thirteen guns of considerable calibre, in addition to the destruction of two ammunition depôts and several military storehouses, observation stations and signalling posts, damage to wharves, moles, and other secondary places. Further a considerable number of casualties are known to have been suffered by the enemy."

During these operations, which are typical of the work done on the Belgian Coast, we lost three ships, the drifter *Great Heart*, the mine-sweeper *Brighton Queen* —an old pleasure steamer —and the armed yacht *Sanda*, the two former by mines and the latter by gun-fire. The loss of the last-named unfortunately involved the death of her commander Lieut-Commander H. T. Gartside-Tipping, who was the oldest naval officer afloat. He had retired from the navy thirty-five years at the outbreak of the war, but in spite of his sixty-six years he rejoined at once, only to meet his death very gallantly in action.

The concluding part of Admiral Bacon's dispatch contains a fine tribute to those who manned the vessels under his command, which was a varied flotilla, including monitors, destroyers, trawlers, drifters, yachts and all sorts of craft converted into mine-sweepers. "Their Lordships will appreciate," he says, "the difficulty attendant on the cruising in company by day and night under war conditions of a fleet of eighty vessels, comprising widely different classes, manned partly by trained naval ratings, but more largely by officers of the Naval Reserve, whose fleet training has necessarily been scant, and by men whose work in life has hitherto been that of deep-sea fishermen.

" The protection of such a moving fleet by the destroyers in waters which are the natural home of the enemy's submarines has been admir-able, and justifies the training and organisation of the personnel of the flotilla. But more remarkable still, in my opinion, is the aptitude shown by the officers and crews of the drifters and trawlers, who in difficult waters, under conditions totally strange to them, have main-tained their allotted stations without a single accident. Moreover, these men under fire have exhibited a coolness well worthy of the personnel of the service, inured by discipline. The results show how deeply sea adaptability is ingrained in the sea-faring race of these islands. "

Upon the development of Dunkirk as a base for British ships most of the coastal work was done from there, and a still closer watch was kept upon the enemy along the coast. In day-

MONITORS BOMBARDING THE BELGIAN COAST BEHIND A SMOKE SCREEN PUT UP BY MOTOR LAUNCHES.

time he dare not show his nose outside harbour, he had too wholesome a respect for the Belgian Coast Patrol, which went up the coast from Dunkirk as far as Zeebrugge almost every day. The B. C. Patrol—as it was known—consisted usually of two large monitors, one small one of the M. class, two mine-sweepers, two drifters, four British destroyers and two French and six M. L. S. for making smoke screens and general utility work. Frequent bombardments of the enemy ports were undertaken by the monitors *Terror*, *Erebus*, *Sir John Moore*, *Lord Clive*, *Gorgon*, *General Wolfe* and *Prince Eugene*. The Germans replied to these pretty hotly with their land batteries, but though their long-range shooting was certainly good, very few casualties occurred on our ships.

A flotilla of coastal motor boats was based on Dunkirk, and some wonderful night-work was put in by them in harrassing the enemy harbours and shipping. Their speed and small size rendered them invaluable for this work. Dunkirk had, as a matter of fact, almost every kind of boat in the navy based there, except battleships and cruisers. The work at this base was varied and interesting, if dangerous.

Dunkirk, too, had the distinction of being the most bombed place in the war; very few nights was it left in peace, and some of those nights are unforgettable for those who were there. The voice of " Mournful Mary," the famous air-raid warning siren, was the nightly call of danger.   In one night alone three hundred and sixty bombs were dropped on the docks and town, but in spite of this and the long-range bombardments from the land the Navy at Dunkirk carried on, and our own last big bombardment from the sea, which was continued for forty-eight hours on end, was one of the main factors in the German's precipitate retreat from the Belgian coast.

CHAPTER VIII.

THE ZEEBRUGGE RAID.

THE action against Zeebrugge on St. George's Day, 1918, was certainly one of the surprises of the war, not only as regards the general public but also for the enemy. Of course, when an operation of this size is undertaken long preparation is necessary, and therefore it is inevitable that the voice of rumour cannot be wholly stilled during all this time, however carefully the secrets may be guarded. You can lock your actual plans up in a safe, but you cannot do the same with the ships necessary for the fulfilment of these plans, nor practise the manœuvres that must be made perfect in a pond in an enclosed park.

Nevertheless the voice of rumour, always, we are told, a lying one, was in the present instance more mendacious than ever. All sorts of wild stories were floating about Dover before the action, especially as the time got nearer, but never once did I hear anything approaching the truth of our objective—the blocking of the Bruges Canal inside the Mole with cement-laden blockships : for it must be remembered that although the wonderful exploits of *Vindictive* in attacking the Mole and the blowing up of the viaduct with the old submarine *C* 3, were the deeds which caught so firm a hold of the imagination of the public, they were, in reality, only " side-shows " to the main idea of the operation—to seal up the pirates in their own nest.

The rumour which gained most credence outside naval circles was that a huge landing was to be attempted along the whole of the Belgian Coast from Nieuport to the Dutch frontier ; even the Germans themselves held this idea, as was shown by the elaborate preparations they had made all along the coast to repel such an attempt.

Before an attack like that in prospect could have a fair chance of success many conditions were necessary, and that uncertain factor, the weather, was not the least important ; moderately calm weather was essential on account of the landing on the Mole, and for the large number of small craft, motor launches and coastal motor boats, to be able to operate in safety, both as regards the smoke screen and the rescue work from the blockships undertaken by the former. The tide had also to be taken into consideration; only at high water could such an operation be carried out, on account of the numerous sandbanks that lie off the Belgian Coast at this part. The wind was the next factor to be considered; everything would depend on that, as with an off-shore wind the smoke screen would have been useless; and lastly there must be no moon. As regards the moon and the tides, these could be reckoned with and the date fixed by calendar, but this done the other factors had to be left in the lap of chance, and not the least uncertain part of this chance was that the weather conditions might be different on the Belgian Coast to those over on the English side, or that these conditions might alter on the way across in the seven hours the flotilla took to do the journey. As a matter of fact the last did happen, and it was a test of intuition on the part of the British commanding officers to meet these changed conditions so that they did not lessen the chances of success.

The main forces that were employed in this operation were assembled at an anchorage in the West Swin, off the Thames Estuary, where the training necessary was carried out and all plans were organised. The training for the smoke screening by the motor launches and coastal motor boats took place at Dover, and was all done in addition to the ordinary patrol work of these vessels. It was as strenuous and exciting a time, this training, as it was necessary, but it bore good fruit, as the brilliant success of the whole action proved.

Those who like statistics may care to know the total number of ships employed in this operation. This number was one hundred and sixty-five, made up as follows :

Motor Launches - - - - -	62
Destroyers - - - - - -	45
Coastal Motor Boats - - - -	24
Monitors - - - - - -	8
Light Cruisers - - - - -	8
Flotilla Leaders - - - - -	7
Blockships - - - - - -	5
Submarines - - - - - -	2
Auxiliary Craft - - - - - (*Iris* and *Daffodil*)	2
Minesweepers - - - - - -	1
Picket Boats - - - - - -	1

All these were British, with the exception of eight destroyers and four motor launches from the French Navy. The personnel of the whole flotilla consisted of 82 officers and 1698 men, mainly drawn from the Grand Fleet, Dover Patrol, and the Harwich Force.

The meeting at a position north of the Goodwin Sands of the main attacking forces from the Swin, and the flotilla of destroyers, submarines, motor launches and coastal motor boats was a fine sight. We—that is the Dover flotilla— were at the position first, and it was an unforgettable sight to see the five blockships headed by *Vindictive* coming slowly up over the horizon. None of them had masts, which added to their strange appearance, and *Vindictive* was fitted with long " brows," or landing gangways, hauled up over her port side, which gave her a very lopsided look.

The whole force then formed into three columns, and it was a wonderful sight, these hundred and sixty-five ships setting out on their great enterprise, headed by the gallant *Vindictive*, who led the centre column, though Vice-Admiral Keyes flew his flag on *Warwick*, which led the starboard column.

We were a motley throng that were now heading for our objective—in broad daylight still—and it was this mixing of large and small craft that made it so impressive, each with its appointed task to perform. Of all the vivid pictures that this night held I think this passage was perhaps the most impressive of all. Our speed was slow, but it was very sure, and the extraordinary part is that the Germans did not know of our coming; so large a number of ships all headed in one direction could not have failed to catch the sight of any aerial patrols had any been up, but our airmen who escorted the flotilla met with no opposition.

As darkness drew on it naturally became much harder to keep station, for a light on any of the ships would have been fatal, though there was little danger of collision, for the same speed was maintained as in daylight.

At a certain position *Sirius* and *Brilliant* left us for Ostend, and what befell them there will be told in another place. On we went towards our objective, and there was a tense feeling of excitement in the air as this great silent black flotilla got nearer and nearer to the enemy harbour. About a mile off the port each ship took up its appointed position for the attack, and the M.L.'s and C.M.B.'s began to make the smoke screen, leaving a gap through which *Vindictive* and the block ships passed.

The schedule time for the operations was exactly a hundred minutes, but so much was going on at once that it will be necessary for me to describe the action in sections, the first of which will be the doings of *Vindictive*.

As I have already said, the attack on the Mole was really intended to take the attention of the enemy away from the blockships. Those who were landed on the Mole were made up of two sections—the storming party who were to engage the enemy, and the demolition party, whose duty it was to do as much damage to war material, guns and buildings as the time would allow. Some of these were to be landed from *Vindictive* herself, and some from the two auxiliaries *Iris II.* and *Daffodil*, the latter ship having also been detailed to push *Vindictive* against the Mole in case her grapnels should not hold her closely enough.

It was a great moment when these three dauntless ships passed through the smoke screen and first sighted the dim outlines of the Mole ahead. Speed was increased to full, and *Vindictive* purposely withheld her fire until emerging from the smoke to avoid discovery until the last possible moment. Then the star shells, that were already brilliantly lighting up the sky, showed her to the enemy, who opened up a raking fire from all the batteries at the sea end of the Mole. So promptly did *Vindictive* reply to this that the two fusillades seemed to ring out almost together. All the guns of the ship that could be brought to bear answered with a deafening roar, and then hell was let loose.

It was exactly one minute past midnight that *Vindictive* was put alongside, and a few minutes later *Daffodil* came up to hold her in position. The fire that poured down on her deck was terrific, and the two leaders of the storming parties were unfortunately killed—Colonel Elliot, of the Royal Marines, and Captain Halahan, who was to lead the bluejackets. However, two other officers took their place in the persons of Captain Chester and Lieut.-Commander Adams.

The landing was made increasingly difficult by the fact that the set of the tide against the Mole caused the ship to roll a good deal, which also broke the foremost Mole anchor. To add

to the already stupendous task before the landing
parties most of the landing gangways had been
smashed by gun-fire as the ship was coming
alongside, and it was found that only two out of
a dozen were fit to be used, and even these two
were swaying and bumping with the rolling of
the ship. Up these very insecure gangways
then this band of men started, officers and men
alike all loaded with Lewis guns, bombs, ammunition and arms. A heavy fire from the enemy
machine guns was kept up on them all the time,
and a drop of some thirty feet was found to be
necessary to get on the Mole from these brows.
Yet in face of these oppositions, each one in
itself enough to upset the whole plan, the landing
party managed to achieve their object.

Here for a moment we must leave them while
we see what happened to *Daffodil* and *Iris II.*,
those stout little ferry boats who had left their
peaceful occupation to face this awful hell.
Both suffered less in approach than did *Vindictive*,
as nearly all the attention of the enemy was
concentrated upon the latter. The *Daffodil* had
a terribly hard task; not only had she to keep
nose on to *Vindictive* to push her against the
Mole as per the original plan, but she found it

necessary to stay there throughout the action on account of the breaking of some of the Mole anchors. This meant that the landing party from the *Daffodil* had to embark over her bows on to the larger ship, and so to the Mole. Without the wonderful handling of *Daffodil* by her C.O., Lieut. H. G. Campbell, very few of the party from *Vindictive* could have landed at all, or, what is even more important still, could have re-embarked after the action.

Meanwhile *Iris II.* was in serious trouble. The tide rip made her bump very heavily, and broke most of her brows before they could be of any use. One was eventually placed in position, and up this went Lieut. Hawkins in a most gallant manner. He secured the Mole anchor, but a second later fell on the Mole shot dead. Equally brave was the conduct of Lieut.-Commander Bradford, who actually climbed to the top of a derrick with a mole anchor on it, leaping on to the parapet and secured it. It was his last act on this earth. In the end it was found quite impossible to get these anchors to hold, so *Iris II.* was forced to drop back alongside *Vindictive* and land her men that way. The larger ship was still suffering heavily, every few seconds fresh showers of shot and shell burst on her deck, and it is a wonder that anyone managed to live there at all. Her 7.5 gun, which had been doing splendid work in return fire, had suffered specially badly, and a Marine gun's crew had been wiped out 'and also a naval crew that took their place. Up in the fighting top a very heroic little party of Marines under Lieut. Rigby (who was killed) was doing splendid work, keeping up a continuous fire with pom-poms and Lewis guns on various targets. Sergeant Finch, one of the few survivors of this band, was awarded the V.C.

It is impossible to mention each heroic act individually on this night, there were too many, but the splendid cool courage of Captain Carpenter, who was in command of *Vindictive*, cannot be allowed to pass unnoticed. This very gallant officer displayed the utmost coolness and skill throughout the action, and, though wounded, carried on to the end of the operations ; never was a V.C. more deserved than his.

It is now time to follow the deeds of the storming and demolition parties that landed on the Mole. These parties, as has been said, were made up of bluejackets and Royal Marines, and special duties had been given to the various units employed, all of which had been exercised on a replica of the Mole. The intention was to land the storming parties in such a position that they could silence first of all the batteries at the seaward end of the Mole, which was of the utmost importance, as they were a great menace to the blockships which were to come in as soon as *Vindictive* had landed her parties to engage the enemy. It was found, however, in the darkness and smoke, that *Vindictive* had overrun her intended position alongside, and this, combined with the difficulties encountered in the actual landing, threw the schedule of time out of its proposed running, and as a result there was only time to silence the main 4″ battery, the incoming blockships unfortunately meeting with very heavy fire from the three guns on the Mole extension.

As soon as the landing parties got on to the Mole they found themselves on a narrow pathway from which was a drop of some fifteen feet to the Mole proper. Along this pathway to seaward the men went and soon came to a lookout station with a range-finder attached to it. This was destroyed with a bomb, and, meeting with no opposition as yet, on the party rushed. Soon they found an iron ladder leading down to the Mole itself, and here they met the enemy. A short but brief encounter ensued, and the Germans gave way before the fierce onslaught of our men, who poured down the ladder, driving the enemy before them. So sudden and sharp was this attack that they had time to cross the Mole (some three hundred feet wide) and to bomb two German destroyers, which were lying at the harbour side, before the crews had time to defend themselves.

Meanwhile a machine gun some hundred yards to seaward was pouring a murderous fire into the ranks of the attacking party, causing many casualties. Another party made their way towards the land end and did great damage with machine guns and bombs upon buildings that were found there, being subjected all the while to a hot fire from the enemy. For the most part the Germans were on the defensive and did the majority of their execution from behind cement gun emplacements. There is no doubt that they were severely "rattled," and the element of surprise was in favour of the attacking party.

A very heavy fire began to be poured upon our men from the destroyers along the harbour side of the Mole and from a strongly fortified zone to which the enemy had retired in strong numbers.

Fresh units were rapidly landing all this while and the fighting was getting fiercer, and it is certainly little less than a miracle that any of those men who fought ever lived to regain their ship again. Altogether these men were on the Mole for about forty-five minutes. I have since examined the landing spot carefully, and can perhaps realise better than one who has not the position that these men found themselves in as soon as they jumped from the scaling ladders. The pathway is very narrow, about 8 feet; to the seaward side is a parapet surmounted by an iron railing, and on the other side another iron railing in front of a 15-foot drop on to the main part of the Mole. Imagine this narrow pathway crowded with men, who were being killed and wounded every second under a terrible fire. The same number of men landing here in daylight would have no easy task, and the more I think of it the more I am filled with sincere admiration and wonder for those who stormed

DESTROYER ACTION OFF DUNKIRK.

the Mole that night. I was quite near *Vindictive* in my own boat, M.L. 314, throughout the action (save for a special " stunt " which I have described in another book) engaged, with other M.L.s, in maintaining the smoke screen, but our work, exciting and dangerous as it was, was a mere sinecure compared to what this landing party went through and those on *Vindictive*. There are some deeds which compel admiration almost beyond adequate speech. This is one of them, and it makes me feel that anything I have said must give but a poor picture of what really happened. It was bloody hell—no milder term will do.

When the recall sounded the officers in charge of the various units did what they could to rally their men. And now came perhaps the hardest and most terrible part of the affair—to get the wounded back on board again. The enemy were still keeping up a devastating fire as these poor fellows were lowered, as tenderly as circumstances would allow, down the scaling ladders, but many a life was lost in this work of mercy before all were aboard.

Some mystery existed at the time as to the fate of Commander Brock, the inventor of the smoke apparatus that did so much to render the operation a success. He was last seen attacking a German gun's crew *with his fists.* It had always been his wish to do this, as he had frequently stated before, and he did it. He was seen to " down " several Huns in this typically English way, and no one saw him after this. He must have met his death while carrying out his dearest wish. He was not originally attached to the storming party, but asked for special permission to land with them for the purposes of investigation. God rest his very gallant soul and all those others whose bodies we left on the Mole that night.

Soon after the party from *Vindictive* had landed on the Mole a mighty roar, that seemed almost to lift the roof of the night, was heard from shorewards. This was a glad sound to the attackers, for it told them that it was now impossible for the enemy to be reinforced from the land, for the explosion they had heard was one they had expected, the submarine blowing up the viaduct that connected the Mole with the shore.

This had been the appointed task of *C* 3, and well she did her work that night. She was under the command of Lieut. R. D. Sandford,

and fitted with special charges of T.N.T. for
the purpose. As she was approaching the viaduct she was seen by the Germans by the light of
the brilliant star shells, and a heavy fire was opened
upon her, and two powerful searchlights picked her
up and kept concentrating upon her. In spite
of this very great danger to her heavy cargo
of explosives the old boat—for she was of an
obsolete pattern—kept steadily on her course,
headed full for her objective. When she was
about three hundred yards away the firing
suddenly ceased and the searchlights were
switched off for a reason which will be explained
shortly. By this time the viaduct was clearly
visible to those on board, and the course was
slightly altered to ensure that she hit at right
angles, which she did a few moments after.
She struck between two rows of piers and rode
up on the girders, lifting her hull bodily several
feet out of the water. She was well in and wedged
as far as her conning tower.

The crew, who were all on deck waiting for
this collision, now lowered the motor skiff in
which they were to make their escape, and the
time fuses were set for the explosion. Not a
hand was raised by the Germans to prevent

this, who could be plainly seen peering over the parapet above at the stranded boat.

As soon as the skiff was manned, and began to make away from the submarine, a heavy fire was opened up upon her, wounding several of her crew, including the commander.

The Germans now began to swarm down the sides of the viaduct on to their " prize," for this was the explanation of the sudden cessation of the firing as the boat approached. The enemy obviously thought that *C* 3 had lost her way and the searchlights were turned off to allow her to wreck herself as she appeared to be going to do.

Then the Huns on this end of the Mole had the nastiest shock of their lives, for while most of them were peering over the parapet watching others clambering over the " captured " vessel, the charges exploded with a terrific roar, blowing the submarine and about a hundred and fifty yards of the viaduct high into the air. Those on board were killed instantly as well as all on that or adjacent parts of the parapet, and the Mole was completely cut off from the shore. *C* 3 had done her work thoroughly when she committed this splendid *felo-de-se*.

The crew in the motor skiff were still in a bad plight, however; the débris of the explosion had gone clean over their heads, luckily they were untouched by this, though the propeller of their boat had been damaged in getting away from the submarine and they had to use oars which made their progress slow. Fire was still being kept up on them spasmodically, and nearly all of that heroic little ship's company were wounded by this time, and their boat holed in several places, only being kept afloat by pumping. Luckily both the searchlights that had been on them were put out of action with the explosion, which proved to be their salvation, for the skiff could not have lived much longer under the fierce fire that was being poured upon them up to this time.

A picket-boat under Lieut.-Commander F. H. Sandford (brother of the Commander of *C* 3) was waiting some little way out to sea and luckily they fell in with this rescue party soon after the explosion, who took them aboard and subsequently transferred them to a destroyer.

It is surely the bitterest jest of Fate that Lieut. Sandford, who had so heroically done his duty in taking in *C* 3 on her dangerous mission, for which he very rightly was awarded the V.C., should die of typhoid fever in England a few months afterwards. He was the second Zeebrugge V.C. to whom fell this terribly unlucky stroke of bad fortune, for Able-Seaman Mackenzie, who got his decoration for his very gallant conduct during the attack on the Mole, where he was one of the landing party, has since died of influenza.

It is perhaps hard to realize that such wonderful acts as the storming of the Mole and the blowing up of the viaduct by *C* 3, were but side-shows to the main operation, as I have said, but such was the case, and to this main operation —the blocking of the Bruges Canal—we must now turn our attention.

The first of the blockships to enter the enemy harbour was *Thetis* with Commander R. S. Sneyd in command. As she approached the end of the Mole she was assisted by rockets fired from *Vindictive* to see her way in and also by Captain Ralph Collins, who was on M.L. 558 (Lieut.-Commander L. S. Chappell, R.N.V.R.); who hailed *Thetis* and gave her the exact bearing from his own observations. When she had rounded the end of the Mole *Thetis* made at once for the large boom which stretched to the shore,

her object being to sink the foremost barge and
thus make the opening wider for the ships that
were to follow her. This she managed to do
by gun fire, but in doing so was unlucky enough
to foul the nets with her propellers, which proved
to be her undoing. She now became unwieldy
and hard to manage, but she continued on
towards the entrance to the canal which was
now plainly visible ahead. When only some three
hundred yards away she had drifted so much
to port that she grounded. She had a strong
list to starboard, for she had met with very
heavy fire as she came in and was badly holed
down by the water-line. She soon began to
settle down and became an easy target with
the Mole guns. Her Commander ordered her
charges to be exploded and here her bottom
was blown out so that her cement laden hull
would settle down quicker, not quite where it
was intended perhaps, but as it subsequently
proved, she was still a useful obstruction, for
the sand silted up here so rapidly that before
many days she had caused a big reef to form
right at the mouth of the canal.

The ship's company manned the one remaining
cutter, which, although overcrowded and holed

in several places, was got away safely and pulled towards M.L.526(Lieut. H. A. Littleton, R.N.V.R.) which was one of the boats for the rescue work, and had followed close on the quarter of *Thetis* right throughout the action.

The next of the blockships to enter the harbour was *Intrepid* under Lieut. S. S. Bonham-Carter. As she approached the Mole she came under very heavy shrapnel fire, but as she rounded the lighthouse most of the guns seemed to be engaged with *Vindictive* and *Thetis* and less attention was paid to her. The fact that the first blockship had sunk one of the boom-barges and carried away the nets was very much in her favour as it allowed her a wider passage in which to manœuvre in this critical part of her course. She managed to make her way well into the Bruges Canal and to get athwart it before the charges were fired to sink her.

The crew took to the boats and were picked up by M.L.282 (Lieut.-Commander P. T. Dean, R.N.V.R.) who had followed her right into the Bruges Canal and who handled his boat in a magnificent manner.

Iphigenia was the third and last of the blockships to enter Zeebrugge harbour and was

MOTOR LAUNCHES RESCUING CREWS OF THE BLOCKSHIPS AT ZEEBRUGGE.

under the command of Lieut. E. W. Billyard-
Leake. She followed close on to *Intrepid* and
on approaching the Mole also came under heavy
shrapnel fire and was lighted up by two powerful
searchlights and by flares, which the enemy
had lighted, but which in reality were to the
advantage of the attacker in facilitating navigation and were rendered useless to the Germans
by our smoke screen. As she approached the
entrance to the canal she was badly hit on the
starboard side, one shell cutting the pipe of the
steam siren, which resulted in the fore part of
the ship being enveloped in steam, which naturally doubled the difficulty of finding the entrance.
She got in, however, but found she was heading
too much for the western pier and to sink her
there would be to leave a gap between the
eastern pier and *Intrepid*. Going full speed astern
her commanding officer fouled a barge and a
dredger and sank them, but he managed to slew
his ship round into the required position and
finally was able to ground on the eastern bank
before he fired his sinking charges. Certainly
a masterly piece of seamanship, for the whole
of the canal entrance was now completely enveloped in thick smoke.

P

The ship's company got away from the vessel in one single cutter, the only remaining boat for use and again M.L.282 came to their rescue, Lieut. Dean having waited after *Intrepid* had been sunk for the coming of *Iphigenia*. The M.L. was forced to go astern out of the canal but finally managed to get clear of the harbour with over a hundred men aboard and under heavy machine-gun fire from the Mole. It was a great feat, and worthy of the V.C. it won.

That the whole operations this night were completely successful was proved at the occupation of these parts some six months later. A large number of German submarines and destroyers were found to be bottled up in Bruges Docks; for the Ostend Canal was not wide enough for them, and Zeebrugge Canal was closed for traffic, thanks to our blockships. The German story that this canal *could* be used for large ships after the night of April 23rd, 1918, was—well, what a good many German stories have proved to be—a lie.

H M S *VINDICTIVE*, APRIL 25TH, 1918

Vindictive
Ap. 25. B.

CHAPTER IX.

THE OSTEND ATTACKS.

THE attack launched against Ostend at the same time as that against Zeebrugge was unfortunately not destined to be crowned with success the first time.

This failure was on no account due to any lack of skill on the part of those who took part in the operation, but to the fact that the Stroom Bank Buoy had been moved by the Germans shortly before the action, whether by coincidence or with any inkling of what was afoot is not known; though probably it was the former, as the attack at Zeebrugge was quite a surprise and if they had had wind of one attempt they would have had of the other.

However, such was the case, and everything went well until the two blockships, *Brilliant* and *Sirius* (the former commanded by Commander A. E. Godsal and the latter by Lieut.-Commander H. N. M. Hardy) were

approaching the charted position of the buoy.
Of this they could see no sign and thinking
that they must be northward of their position
they continued on their course for a couple of
minutes or so and eventually sighted the buoy
ahead. Not knowing of its altered position
they set their course for the harbour mouth
on the original bearing. The smoke screen was
very thick and *Sirius* was compelled to keep
very close station on *Brilliant.*

They now began to come under heavy fire
from the shore batteries, and when the piers
to the entrance to Ostend harbour should have
been in sight breakers were heard on the starboard
bow, which a moment later became dimly visible.
The helm was immediately put hard over, but
it was too late and *Brilliant* grounded before the
engines had time to go astern. *Sirius,* who was
close behind, at once put her helm over and even
managed to check her speed a little by reversing
her engines, but the ship, already badly damaged
by gunfire and sinking, was very slow to answer
and collided with the port quarter of *Brilliant*
and then followed her on to the sand.

Both ships were now in a bad plight ; it was
impossible to get off the sands and they were

but stationary targets for the enemy guns. It was very obvious that something had gone wrong, and that they had missed their mark, so it was deemed advisable to blow the bottoms out of them to save them falling into the hands of the Germans.

Meanwhile the rescue M.L.s had come up alongside the stranded ships and proceeded with the work of taking off the crews. Commander Hamilton Benn, R.N.V.R. in M.L.532 had the misfortune to damage the bows of his boat alongside *Brilliant* owing to the dense smoke, and was obliged to retire as he was in imminent danger of sinking; but his place was taken by M.L.276 under Lieut. R. Bourke, R.N.V.R., who, with Lieut K. R. Hoare, R.N.V.R. in M.L.283, managed to get all the survivors from both ships, though subjected all the while to a raking fire from the shore batteries.

This work of rescue by the M.L.s was a notable one, as in this case there was no diverting attack as at Zeebrugge Mole, and all the batteries and firing parties ashore were concentrated on the two stranded blockships, which were lit up all the time by searchlights.

It was certainly the worst of bad luck that

this eleventh hour removal of the Stroom Bank Buoy should have caused this failure, for aerial photos taken a few days after established the fact that had the buoy been in position as charted the ships would have made the harbour entrance accurately.

It was the fortune of war and due to no fault on the attackers' part, and soon after this—on the night of May 9th-10th—a second, and this time successful, operation was undertaken against Ostend.

For this, *Vindictive*, her honourable scars of her former fight patched up and her hull filled with cement, was chosen as one of the block-ships; and *Sapho*, another old cruiser, was got ready for a similar purpose. The weather, the few days previous to this second attack, was very bad and precluded air reconnaissance, which was very necessary in view of the enemy having made any preparations against another attempt to block the harbour, until the day of the coming action, when an airman discovered that all the buoys off Ostend had been removed. This move on the enemy's part, only discovered at the last moment, was a serious one and counter measures had to be adopted to defeat it. Accordingly a special calcic-phosphide buoy had to be prepared to be laid by a motor craft as a departure point for the blockships.

These operations against Ostend were worked from Dunkirk on both occasions, and were carried out under the very able leadership of Commodore Hubert Lynes, the S.N.O. at Dunkirk.

Just before dark we assembled in Dunkirk Roads and the M.L.s and monitors proceeded to their appointed stations. For this action special monitors were placed close inshore as well as to seaward, to carry on a strong bombardment of the German batteries to the west of Ostend. These inshore monitors came under very heavy fire, as I know from personal experience. It was a most impressive sight as the M.L.s went towards the shore making their smoke screen. The dim outline of the enemy coast could be seen faintly, till suddenly illuminated by a burst of flame as the batteries opened on us and the splash of the shells in the water around us told us that the Germans had already got our range.

The smoke screen off the harbour was acting well, the wind was good and the sea calm ;

in fact all was in favour of success as regards climatic conditions, and it was an unlucky fate that cut down these chances by half; for soon after the start the *Sapho* burst a boiler and her speed was at once reduced to a maximum of six knots, which rendered her participation in the operation that night out of the question.

This serious accident, coming at the eleventh hour, required careful consideration as to whether it was advisable to proceed with the operation or abandon it. However, it was decided to carry on with *Vindictive* alone.

After the removal of the buoys off Ostend a report had come through that nine German destroyers had been seen proceeding out of the harbour and some resistance was expected, but nothing occurred. The special starting off buoy from the blockships was laid without let or hindrance. Star shells and " flaming onions " were fired from the coast as the flotilla approached, but these seemed to be more part of the enemy's searching routine than anything. No patrol craft of any sort were sighted. It is an extraordinary thing that the Germans, especially on this occasion after the first attack, had no preparations against surprise from the sea, beyond

H M S *QUEEN*, TRAWLERS AND DRIFTERS,
TARANTO

By the courtesy of the Imperial War Museum

been added, they saw the British in the light of deliverers.

At Gaza our monitors assisted the left flank of the army with heavy bombardments and were the means of that place being evacuated before the arrival of the victorious army. The naval forces were under the command of Rear-Admiral Jackson and worked from a base at Ismailah, in Egypt.

Some interesting side lights of these operations are given in a letter I received from a naval officer who took part in them, "I can now tell you," he wrote, "some of the lighter side of our life out here without fear of being shot by the censor. The bombardment of Gaza was quite weird. We always began in the very early morning, about an hour before daylight. It gradually got lighter and lighter as we strafed the gentle Turk till the sun rose above the hills like a ball of fire. Then all at once the land completely disappeared as if by magic. It was quite uncanny, but reasonable of explanation. Not being eagles we couldnt look in the face of such a sun as we get out here. So for several hours we ceased firing till the sun rose higher, when the land gradually came into view again, when we carried on.

R

" The capture of Alexandretta, a small harbour along the coast, had a quaint touch about it. Intimation was sent to the Turks that the place was to be surrendered or blown to hell. This the Turks refused to do, but offered no resistance. Accordingly a scratch crew was got together, to man a ship's boat to go ashore, which consisted of one Lieutenant, cooks, drifter hands and marines. No one opposed the landing and the party proceeded to the centre of the town and hoisted the Union Jack over the Government Building, to the intense interest of the local inhabitants, while the Turkish garrison merely looked on with a bored indifference! So when you read in the paper that ' The port of Alexandretta was captured by our naval forces ' you can picture the scene. Everything was there, even to the ' chorus of villagers,' in true comic opera style !

" On another occasion the Turk had his leg very neatly pulled. During the retreat near Gaza two barge loads of ' dummy troops ' set out from Ismailah accompanied by a small flotilla of various craft. These were members of the Egyptian Labour Corps and at night were ' secretly ' landed in front of the flying Turks.

MONITOR M 31 BOMBARDING GAZA AT DAWN

By the courtesy of the Imperial War Museum

This landing was a great stunt, boat load after boat load was put ashore and with a light ' accidentally ' shown on frequent occasions for the benefit of the enemy outposts, who were known to be watching. Then with *real* secrecy these Labour Corps men were re-embarked and towed away. The next day the Turks hurried up several regiments to search for the landing party that were thought to be ambushed for a secret attack in the rear. Of course there was not a man there, but it made them very uneasy till they discovered how they had been ' had ! '

" Have you ever heard of camels being used in connection with mine-sweeping ? It sounds like a yarn, but when I was on the Suez Canal I saw them for myself. It was not exactly mine-sweeping but next door to it. The M.L.s swept the water of the Suez Canal, but a camel ' sweep ' of two flat boards was run over the sandy approaches of the canal, so that any footprints made in the night would be clearly visible, for the Turks had a trick of bringing mines by land and dropping them into the water during the dark hours.

" Some of the harbours out here would amuse you, but I think Tricasse is the most comic, it is a little place in the " heel " of Italy where the M.L.s used to shelter at times. The harbour is no larger than a lock and six M.L.s could just squeeze in abreast, though the last one had a devil of a job to get in! When I was on the Otranto-Albania barrage patrol I was interested in the towers that are built along the coast on the Italian side. They are something like the Martello Towers one sees on the S.E. coast in England. These towers out here were built by the Crusaders against the Turks, well, we are new Crusaders still fighting the Turks for the possession of the Holy Land, though we use tanks instead of towers these days.

" All the M.L.s out here are camouflaged with broad white stripes painted over the dark-blue grey. They look weird, but effective."

Of all the naval operations in the Mediterranean the landing of the Army at Gallipoli Peninsula in the Dardanelles in 1915, was the greatest. For several months previously the Turkish forts and positions were subjected to severe bombardments from the sea, in which we were assisted by French ships. The vessels that played a leading part in this were the *Queen Elizabeth, Cornwallis, Triumph, Agamemnon*

Irresistible, Vengeance and *Albion* ; with the three old French battleships, the *Gaulois, Bouvet* and *Suffren*; with later on the *Ocean,* the *Prince George,* the *Lord Nelson* and the French *Charlemagne* also took part in the attacks.

All this was not done without loss to ourselves, for the *Irresistible* and the *Ocean* were sunk by drifting mines and the *Inflexible* and *Gaulois* badly damaged by the guns from the forts. But it is not to tell the story of these bombardments but of the great " glorious failure " of the landing, to which they were but the prelude, that is my intention now.

The troops that were to land on the Peninsula had assembled at Mudros and the adjacent islands in readiness some time before the landing took place. Although this is always spoken of as " the landing " it was in reality several landings in different places and with these we must naturally deal separately.

Two main landings took place, one at a point north of Gaba Tepe and another at the southern end of the Peninsula, while in addition to these a third landing was made by the French at Kum Kale on the Asiatic side. The landing at Gaba Tepe—known to most as Anzac Cove—

was a single landing, but that to the southern was divided into several sub-landings as follows : " Y " beach, about 4 miles N.W. of Cape Tekeh, " X " beach three miles further on, " W " beach between Cape Tekeh and Cape Helles, " V " beach towards Sedd-el-Bahr, and " S " beach at Eski-Hissarlik Point.

The landing at Gaba Tepe was under the charge of Rear-Admiral C. F. Thursby, who had with him the battleships *London*, *Queen*, and *Prince of Wales* carrying troops, with the *Majestic*, *Triumph* and the cruiser *Bacchante* which covered the landing by gunfire, while a flotilla of destroyers, the seaplane carrier *Ark Royal*, the balloon ship *Mancia* and fifteen trawlers completed his squadron.

The night of April 24th-25th was calm and very clear, with a bright moon which had just set, when our ships approached the land about 3 a.m. The troops were landed in two trips, the operation taking about half an hour. The preliminary bombardment was withheld at the last moment as it was hoped that there might be a chance of taking the enemy by surprise, and in silence our troop-laden vessels crept inshore. Just as the men were getting ready to land the Turks discovered

SEA-PLANE FLYING OVER DAMASCUS

By the courtesy of the Imperial War Museum

the presence of the ships and a sharp fire was at once opened, upon both boats and beach. Nothing, however, was to stop these undaunted men; it was a fight with the dawn, for with the advent of daylight casualties among the attackers were certain to be heavier. Many men were hit before they got into the small boats and others were never to reach the shore, but the rest carried on in a truly gallant fashion. The fire from the heights above became murderous by daylight, but by this time the Australians had established themselves on the beach, and the charge in which they stormed the cliff and captured the ridge above is world famous. Of this charge the Admiral in charge of the whole operations, Vice-Admiral J. M. de Robeck, wrote, " At Gaba Tepe the landing and dash of the Australian Brigade for the cliffs was magnificent —nothing could stop such men. The Australian and New Zealand Army Corps in this, their first battle, set a standard as high as that of any army in history, and one of which their country-men have every reason to be proud."

On the following day the landing of troops, guns and stores continued. This was most strenuous work, as the enemy kept up a constant shrapnel fire, from well concealed batteries which were extremely difficult to locate. At intervals bursts of fire from enemy ships in the Narrows interfered still more with the work, but these attacks were not of long duration, as the fire from our own covering naval forces always caused the enemy to retire. The Turks on land, too, tried several counter attacks, but in spite of their being supported by the heavy shrapnel fire they made no impression on our line, and by the evening of the 26th our position here was securely in our keeping.

The landing at the southern end of the Peninsula was under the command of Rear-Admiral R. E. Wemyss, whose squadron consisted of the battleships *Swiftsure*, *Cornwallis*, *Implacable*, *Albion*, *Prince George*, *Lord Nelson*, *Vengeance* and *Goliath*, the cruisers *Dublin*, *Euryalus*, *Talbot* and *Minerva* with half a dozen mine-sweepers and fourteen trawlers.

The first troops that landed at " Y " beach were the King's Own Scottish Borderers, who had proceeded from Mudros in the cruisers *Amethyst* and *Sapphire* and the transports *Southland* and *Braemar Castle*. So good a protective screen was put up by the *Goliath* that these troops

RETALIATION

Merchant ship engaging a U-boat.

managed to gain not only the beach but also
the top of the high cliffs practically without
opposition. A detachment of the Royal Naval
Division followed, and also gained the top of
the cliffs ; but here both forces met with strong
opposition, for once having gained this position
the covering fire from the sea was of little assistance and after twenty-four hours severe and
almost incessant fighting it was considered impossible to join up with the landing party at " X "
beach, which had been the original intention,
so orders were given to re-embark. Casualties
had been heavy and it was but a depleted band
of fighters who were taken off by the *Goliath*,
Sapphire, *Amethyst*, *Dublin* and *Talbot*. This
re-embarkation was very finely carried out by
the beach personnel and covered by the barrage
fire from the battleships, which prevented the
enemy, with the exception of a few snipers,
reaching the cliff edge. Both operations were
conducted by Lieut.-Commander Adrian St. V.
Keyes, of whom General Sir Ian Hamilton
reported—" The success of the landing on ' Y '
beach was largely due to his good services.
When circumstances compelled the force landed
there to re-embark, this officer showed exceptional

resource and leadership in successfully conducting that difficult operation."

The debarkation at " X " beach was more successful ; here the Royal Fusiliers were landed from the *Implacable* with very few casualties. The battleship came very close inshore and opened up so fierce a fire that the Turks retreated after some resistance, but made a strong counter-attack when our men got ashore, which pre-vented them gaining possession of the original objective—a certain hill behind the landing-place—though they were able to entrench them-selves on the beach and later on to join hands with the party from " W " beach.

The landing at the latter was carried out by the Lancashire Fusiliers from the cruiser *Euryalus*. A heavy fire was kept up here from the covering ships up to the last moment before landing, though without doing the damage to the wire-entanglements that had been hoped for, and the troops on landing were met with a hot fire from machine-guns, pom-poms and rifles. The formation of the beach at this spot was strongly in favour of the defenders, the landing spot being commanded by sloping cliffs which made ideal positions for trenches and gun emplace-

ments. There was one weakness, however, in
the enemy's position, it was just possible to
get on to the rocks and enfilade the more important defences. Of this our men took full advantage and a landing on these rocks was effected
with great skill and bravery, in spite of the heavy
fire, men hacking away the wire, which in some
cases was concealed beneath the water, with
axe and bayonet. Some enemy maxims, which
were concealed in the cliff and were sweeping
the main beach, were brilliantly taken by bayonet
charge after desperate fighting.

This was a great help to the main body, which,
although still losing heavily, managed to gain
possession of the beach and the approaches to it.
Of the importance of this Admiral de Robeck
reported : " This success cannot be over-esti-
mated ; ' W ' and ' V ' beaches were the only
two of any size in this area, on which troops,
other than infantry, could be disembarked, and
failure to capture this one might have had
serious consequences, as the landing at ' V '
was held up. The beach was being continuously
sniped and a fierce infantry battle was carried
on round it throughout the entire day and the
following night. It is impossible to exalt too

highly the service rendered by the 1st Battalion Lancashire Fusiliers in the storming of the beach ; the dash and gallantry were superb. Not one whit behind in devotion to duty was the work of the beach personnel, who worked untiringly throughout the day and night, landing troops and stores under continual sniping. The losses due to rifle and machine-gun fire sustained by the boats' crews, to which they had not the satisfaction of being able to reply, bear testimony to the arduous nature of the service. During the night the enemy attacked continuously and it was not until 1 p.m. on the 26th, when ' V ' beach was captured, that our position might be said to be secure. The work of landing troops, guns, and stores continued throughout this period and the conduct of all left nothing to be desired."

The anticipations that " V " beach would be the most difficult to capture were fully justified. It possessed all the advantages to the enemy that " W " beach had, and in addition the flanks were strongly guarded by the old castle and village of Seddul Bahr to the eastward, and perpendicular cliffs to the westward. The whole of the foreshore was a mass of barbed wire entanglements which also extended under the sea. Overlooking the beach were the ruins of the old barracks, a spot which was ideal for sharp shooters and maxims. The whole position formed a huge amphitheatre with the beach as the stage.

This was subjected to a very heavy preliminary bombardment, but when the first boats cast off from the transports they were met with a murderous fire from rifles and machine-guns. It was impossible to land on the flanks here and a frontal attack was necessary, with the result that nearly all those who went in the first trip were either killed or wounded; only a mere handful managing to reach the shore. In several of the boats all the occupants were killed, or so severely hurt as to render them incapable of carrying on. One boat was smashed to pieces and disappeared altogether and in others but two or three were left, and even of these who managed to scramble ashore some were killed on the barbed wire or as they were struggling up the beach.

As soon as the boats had left, a preconceived scheme for landing an additional force was put into action. This was by running the transport

River Clyde ashore at the eastern end of the beach where she could form a breakwater for the landing of supplies subsequently. She was filled with troops also and had been specially fitted out for this occasion. Originally a collier, large ports had been cut in her side and gangways built through which the men could reach a string of lighters which were to form a floating bridge to the beach. When the *River Clyde* grounded these boats were at once run out ahead of her, but unfortunately, owing to the difficulties of working, they failed to reach their proper positions, with the result that a gap was left between two of the boats which was too broad for the men to jump. Some tried to land by leaping from the lighter in position into the sea and wading ashore, but owing to the fierce fire that was being kept up this proved too costly a method, men were being killed like flies, and orders were given for the disembarkation to cease for a time and for the soldiers to remain in the *River Clyde*, where they were in comparative safety from the rifles and machine-guns.

Efforts were still made, however, to get the bridge of boats into position and to assist in this work the commanding officer of the ship, Commander Edward Unwin, himself left the bridge and stood up to his waist in water under a very heavy fire. He worked on till he was exhausted by cold and exposure and was obliged to return to the ship. Here he was wrapped up in blankets till he recovered to some degree, when he returned, against doctor's orders, to his task and " stuck it " till it was completed. He was wounded three times and after treatment on board he once again left the ship in a lifeboat to save some wounded men who were lying in shallow water near the shore.

In the task of getting the lighters into position he was heroically assisted by two midshipmen, W. S. A. Malleson, R.N., and G. L. Drewry, R.N.R., both of whom volunteered to swim with lines from lighter to lighter after they had swung out of position, while Able Seaman Williams and Seaman R. W. R. Samson also worked with the lighters, the former until killed and the latter until badly wounded. These five men all received the V.C.

The bridge to the shore, though now in position, could not be used by the troops, as anyone venturing on it was instantly shot by the snipers, who were keeping a special watch upon it.

Consequently it was decided to postpone the landing of the remainder of the troops until a cover of darkness would protect them. During the day a brisk fire was kept up on the enemy from the covering ships and the maxims on the *River Clyde*, protecting, as far as was possible, the men who were already on the beach under what rather scanty shelter they could find.

As soon as darkness set in the troops on the collier were successfully landed and then the real battle for possession of the beach and the village and the cliffs above it began. The chief regiments that took part in this great struggle were the Dublin Fusiliers, the Munsters and the Hampshires. The fight went on till half past one in the morning, when, supported by gunfire from the *Albion*, our men had carried a hill that held the key to the situation. The ship then ceased fire and the main hill with the old castle on the top was stormed and carried by our men.

The taking of this position cleared the enemy from the neighbourhood of " V " beach, the capture of which called for a display of the utmost bravery and perseverance from the officers and men of both the Navy and the Army

A NIGHT ESCORT

Destroyers convoying a troopship to France.

and—to use the words of Admiral de Robeck— "that they successfully accomplished their task bordered on the miraculous."

There was also a landing of half a company of the Dublin Fusiliers slightly to the east of " V " beach on a spot known as the Camber, with the intention of attacking the village of Seddul-Bahr, but on account of the narrowness of the approach they were unable to achieve their object and were compelled to re-embark after suffering very heavy losses. This action was subsidiary to the " V " beach action, and the last of our landings was that on " S " beach. Here the South Wales Borderers and the Royal Engineers landed in boats from the *Cornwallis* under a covering fire from the *Lord Nelson*. Compared with some of the other positions little opposition was encountered and the beach and cliffs were soon in the possession of our men, and they were able to entrench themselves before the enemy counter-attacked, which attacks were easily beaten off with the assistance of the fire from the battleships.

The landing on the Asiatic side, at Kum Kale, was undertaken by the French troops, under the covering fire from their own ships.

T

This was carried out in order to prevent the enemy occupying positions on this coast whence he could bring fire on the landings on the other side. It was also hoped that by holding this position it might be possible to deal more effectually with the Turkish gun emplacements to the east of Kum Kale, which commanded " W " and " S " beaches. After a heavy preliminary bombardment the French managed to land their force by the afternoon with few casualties, but when they advanced towards Yeni Shehr, which was their immediate objective, they met with a heavy fire from concealed trenches, which held up the advance.

During the night the Turks made many counterattacks, all of which were beaten off, in fact, in one of them 400 Turkish prisoners were taken. On the following day it became apparent that no advance could be undertaken without large reinforcements and, as they were not forthcoming at the time, the force re-embarked without much opposition.

This completed the landings, which are unique, alike in the annals of both navy and army, except for the second great landing four miles south of Anzac Cove at Suvla Bay on August

7th when again, as Sir Ian Hamilton said, the Navy played father and mother to the Army. During the whole time of the occupation the Navy was responsible for feeding, clothing and supplying with war materials the men that held their positions on this desolate coast, against such awful odds, and also took them off again when their long and horror-strewn vigil was over, in that wonderful silent evacuation, carried out so successfully that the enemy were not aware that our army had withdrawn until the following day.

The full story of Gallipoli belongs to the military side of the history of the war and how near this became to being a great success has now come to light. Of the Navy's share in this great undertaking we have seen, and whatever the final result may have been no finer deeds of heroism have been performed in either service than those which took place at the great landing on this bleak iron coast.

CHAPTER XI.

THE NAVY IN THE EAST.

THE name of Baghdad conjures up visions of Caliph Haroun al Raschid and the Arabian Nights more readily than of the British Navy, and when we hear of an S.N.O. Baghdad, and monitors using this ancient city of romance as a Base, some five hundred miles up a river, it emphasises the truth of the rather well-worn, but in this case applicable, phrase : " The far flung battle-line."

Before speaking of naval activities in these strange waters it may be as well to give some idea of the Tigris and adjacent country. I cannot do this better than by quoting from a letter I received from the illustrator of this book written from Baghdad.

" The statement often made that Mesopotamia is a vast desert through which run two great rivers, bare but for the palm trees on their banks and flat as a pancake, is true as far as it goes. It is possible, however, to picture a land entirely different from Mesopotamia and still stick to this description. I have met countless men out here who have told me that they had built up in their minds a wrong conception of the country and a wrong idea of its character simply by letting their imagination get to work on insufficient data.

" To begin with the word desert generally suggests sand. People who have been to Egypt or seen the Sahara naturally picture a sandy waste with accompanying oases, palms and camels. Mesopotamia, however, is a land of clay, of mud, uncompromising mud. The Thames and Medway saltings at high tide stretching away to an infinity in every direction—this is the picture that I carry in my mind of the riverside country between Basra and Amara. No blue limpid waters by Baghdad's shrines of fretted gold, but pea soup or *café au lait*. Even the churned foam from a paddle-wheel is *café au lait*, with what a bluejacket contemptuously referred to as ' a little more of the *au lait* ! ' At a distance it can be blue, gloriously blue, by reflection from the sky, but it will not bear close examination. It is perfectly true that the country is as 'flat as a pancake' in original formation, but the pieces of ancient irrigation systems, to say nothing of buried cities--Babylon is quite mountainous for Mesopotamia—make it a very bumpy plain in places.

"Of the two great rivers, Tigris and Euphrates, the banks of the latter are more wooded and picturesque and the former is busier. The backwaters, creeks and side channels of both are exceedingly beautiful, and here one can get a glimpse of the fertility that must have belonged to Mesopotamia when it was a net-work of streams and when forests abounded within its borders.

"Centuries of neglect and the blight of the unspeakable Turk, have dealt badly with this country. It is indeed a Paradise Lost, and it will be many years before it is a Paradise Regained.

"In the creeks the water is much clearer than in the main rivers, as they deposit the silt when they flow more placidly than in the turmoil of the main streams. Oranges, bananas, lemons and mulberries abound, with vines trailing from palm to palm in some of the backwaters. In one narrow waterway near Basra, a sort of communication trench between two canals, I saw orange bushes overhanging the water, and growing with them some plant with great white bells.

"The natives use a curious craft here—or rather one of their curious craft—called a goufa. Talk of standardisation! Here is a boat standardised before the time of Sennacherib! Assyrian sculptures in the British Museum show this boat in use exactly as it is to-day, and although we have no records of it, it was probably in use for ages previously. Noah, possibly, had one as a dinghy to the Ark! The goufa is made like a basket and then coated with bitumen. It is a delightful shape and a fascinating colour; sort of milky-blue-grey, somewhere between the colour of an elephant and an old lead vase."

It is certainly a far call from a battleship to a goufa, but the navy included both, for these basket-boats on the Tigris were all numbered and pressed into service, some as carriers for our ships and others, under the direction of the Inland Water Transport (known under the nickname of "Kitchener's Navy"). Another native boat in Mesopotamia used for naval purposes was the bellum, a long narrow craft specially built for the swift currents of the Tigris and Euphrates. These are propelled by oar and paddle or punted in shallow water, while they also carry sails. They were largely used in the operations in these waters for carrying infantry, and sometimes two were lashed together and a platform built in between to carry a machine-gun. A subsequent development was the armoured bellum, fitted with steel plates for protection against rifle bullets.

The largest native craft on these rivers were the mahailahs, boats about the size of a fishing smack, which looked something like a cross between a Viking ship and Noah's Ark, for they had high prows and sterns and house like deck cabins. Mahailahs were known as " The Royal Yachts of Nebuchadnezzar." Several of these craft were converted into hospital ships for naval and military use and served this purpose very well.

So much for the native boats and it will be as well to continue the list of the " Dramatis Personae " with something about our own ships which operated in this unusual naval war zone. Below the narrows were the sloops *Odin* and

PARADISE REGAINED   H M S *MANTIS* ON THE
TIGRIS

By the courtesy of the Imperial War Museum

Espeigle, while the subsequent operations were carried on by the monitors *Tarantula*, *Moth* and *Mantis*. Supporting these were the " Fly " class gunboats, specially built for these shallow waters, and several motor launches (distinct from the ordinary M.L.s).

Navigation in these rivers was always difficult, owing to the sharp bends and the numerous shifting sandbanks and I doubt if ever in this war naval craft operated under more adverse conditions with such conspicuous success.

The campaign in Mesopotamia has been very aptly described as an amphibious one, for owing to the frequent floodings of the rivers and the many canals or cuts made for irrigation purposes the whole country is under water to a large extent for nearly half the year, so that the Army, as well as the Navy, had to look to the water for means of transit.

In our advance in May, 1915, when the successful attack was made on the Turks above Kurnah (which is situated at the junction of the two rivers and is the reputed site of the Garden of Eden) the enemy held the only dry portions of the country, small sand hills in the midst of the floods, and these the infantry had

U

to attack for the most part in boats, under the covering fire from the naval forces in the river. In armoured bellums the soldiers approached, getting what cover they could from the tall reeds that grew in this marshland, and then leapt ashore and stormed the trenches. This attack was completely successful and soon the Turk was in full flight up the Tigris with the Navy-Army in pursuit. Two launches went in front as mine-sweepers, followed by the sloops and the smaller craft, with the soldiers in stern paddlers in the rear. These stern paddlers were extraordinary craft, rather like double-decked houseboats with a thing like an antiquated waterwheel on the stern to supply the motive power.

The Turkish Army was being towed in barges with a small gun-boat, the *Marmaris*, leading the procession, but in spite of their long start our forces gradually drew up and as soon as they came within range the sloops opened fire upon them. The Turks saw that further flight was useless; again and again the naval gunners were finding their marks on the barges or the small steamers towing them, so they suddenly drew into the bank to await their captors. The *Marmaris* was eventually set on fire by her own crew, though her guns were afterwards found to be still serviceable to us. This surrender took place at Ezra's Tomb of Biblical fame, and the following day our forces proceeded up the river and took the town of Amara. Altogether the Turks in this operation lost nearly 4000 men, killed, wounded or prisoners, as well as all their steamers, barges and other craft, together with ammunition and stores.

Although the main river operations took place on the Tigris, before we speak of the further advance of the Navy up that river it will be well to mention the capture of Nasiriyah up the Euphrates and the share the Navy had in this, which took place about a month after the surrender just described. Nasiriyah was an important Turkish base and to reach it the force had to cross Hammar Lake, a large but shallow stretch of water with a difficult and winding channel. All the naval craft capable of operating under such conditions that could be got together in the time required were three stern-paddlers, the armoured launch *Sumana* and two horse-boats each carrying a 4.7 gun.

This small but intrepid flotilla, which was led by the *Shushan*, a very ancient stern-paddler, met with little opposition until they had passed through Hammar Lake, breaking down the dam that the enemy had placed across the entrance to the Euphrates, where two Turkish motor-launches (built by Thornycrofts) opened fire on the advancing force with pom-poms. These soon retired under the fire of our 4.7's and our force advanced to support the army who were making their way along the banks, with difficulties of their own to encounter.

After the occupation of Suk-y-Sheyukh the main Turkish position of Asani was carried after stiff fighting and the flotilla proceeded up to Nasiriyah, which the Turks finally evacuated after a little show of opposition on the part of one of the Turkish motor launches (one had already been sunk by the enemy with the hope of blocking the channel). This last launch was set on fire by the shells from the *Shushan*, whereupon her crew ran her ashore and abandoned her.

To return to the Tigris. Our forces, both naval and military, had pushed on, capturing Kut-el-Amara by the end of September and the naval flotilla was lying about two miles below Ctesiphon, when the Army fell back in that disastrous retirement which ended in General

Townshend and his men being besieged at Kut. In this retreat the Navy was unlucky enough to lose two armed launches, the *Comet* and the *Spartan*, as well as the first of the specially designed class, the *Firefly*, which ran aground and had to be abandoned.

Several attempts were made to relieve Kut, but they were unfortunately unavailing, and in these the Navy played their part on one occasion, in a singular manner, when in Biblical fashion they showed a Pillar of Fire by Night to guide the soldiers across the trackless waste. This was the searchlight of a monitor with the beam in a vertical position behind the advancing troops, from which they were able to get a bearing to lead them to their objective ahead. At another time a desperate attempt was made by the Navy to bring food to the beleaguered garrison (which held out till April 1916). This was made a few weeks before the surrender, when the steamer *Julnar* was fitted up with steel plates and laden with foodstuffs in an endeavour to get through the Turkish forces on both sides of the river. It was a plucky attempt, one of the most plucky of the war, but it was doomed to failure. The little ship came under very heavy fire as she approached the enemy lines and the C.O., Lieut. H. O. B. Tirman, was killed, still she kept on, Lieut.-Commander C. H. Cowley, R.N.V.R., taking his captain's place till he too was killed as he was steering the ship through the most dangerous and critical part of the river; with the result that the *Julnar* ran aground and fell into the hands of the Turks. Both these officers were awarded posthumous V.C.s.

A fortnight later the garrison of Kut were forced to surrender and for a period activities, especially naval ones, died down, and it was not until December that the great advance began which led to the complete rout of the Turks, and finally to the re-capture of Kut and the capture of Baghdad in March, 1917.

The advance up the Tigris commenced on December 13th, 1916, the naval forces being under the command of Captain Wilfred Nunn, who had four monitors, *Tarantula*, *Moth*, *Mantis* and *Gnat*, and among other craft, the newly built flotilla of " Fly " boats —*Butterfly*, *Sandfly*, *Snakefly*, *Greenfly*, *Gadfly*, *Stonefly*, *Mayfly*, *Waterfly* and *Flycatcher*, and latterly the *Firefly*, which was re-captured by us in the advance.

The situation early in the year was summed up by the S.N.O. in his despatch : " On the left bank our forces were held up by the Turks in the extremely strong Sannaiyat position, while on the right bank we had advanced much further up the river. Operations proceeded in a most satisfactory manner, and early in February our forces were in possession of the right bank as far as to the westward of Kut-el-Amara, with bridges over the Hai, large numbers of prisoners having been taken, guns captured, and heavy losses inflicted on the enemy.

" After intense bombardment, in which the gunboats co-operated, a successful assault of the Sannaiyat position was made on Feb. 22nd, and a footing obtained. During the night following dummy attempts were made to cross the river in various places above Sunnaiyat and just before daybreak covering parties were rowed across the Tigris near Shumran in pontoons, a surprise landing effected, and a bridge thrown across. The whole Turkish position was manifestly becoming untenable, and they commenced a general retreat, which developed later into a rout."

The next day the naval forces moved up the

river to Kut-el-Amara, to find it deserted and
in ruins. A force landed and took formal possession of the town, the scene of so much heroic
suffering on the part of General Townshend
and his men, and when our ships went on up
the river the British flag was once again flying
over this city of bitter memories.

"I received a message," wrote Captain Nunn,
"from General Maude asking me to co-operate
in pursuing the retreating Turks and inflict
as much damage as possible. I proceeded
at full speed in *Tarantula* leading *Mantis* and
Moth with *Gadfly* and *Butterfly* following at
their utmost speed."

The naval force captured the small town of
Bghailah without opposition, taking some two
hundred prisoners and several guns. Above this
place the Turkish Navy came into action to
support its flying Army. The enemy ships opened
up a hot fire at the pursuers, chiefly from the
armed steamer *Pioneer* and the *Firefly*, the
ex-H.M. ship. The running fight was kept up
and our ships were under heavy fire from the
land, where the Turks had left special guns to
cover their retreat, and the casualties on our side
were beginning to be pretty severe: "There

THE NAVY IN BAGHDAD
Exhibited at the Royal Academy in 1919
By the courtesy of the Imperial War Museum

were casualties in all three ships," says the despatch, " the *Moth*, which was magnificently handled by Lieut.-Commander C. H. A. Cartwright, who was himself wounded, had three officers severely wounded, and two men killed and eighteen wounded. The ship was hit eight times by shell and the upper deck and funnels riddled by bullets. The Quartermaster and Pilot in the conning-tower of the *Mantis* were killed, but the prompt action of her Captain, Commander Bernard Buxton, saved her from running ashore."

The ships had now passed the enemy rearguard and large numbers of the retreating Turks were on their starboard beam. Fire was at once opened on them with all guns that would bear, including heavy and light guns, pompoms, maxims and rifles. At so short a range this did enormous execution, the enemy being too demoralised to reply, except in a very few cases. We were able to shoot down some of the gun teams, and these pieces fell into the hands of our advancing troops.

The enemy ships ahead were within easy range and several surrendered including the *Sumana*, which had been left in Kut during the siege and captured at the fall of that place.

x

Soon after this the large steamer *Basra*, which was manned by German gunners, surrendered on coming under heavy fire from the *Tarantula*. The *Firefly* continued to put up a sporting fight, but it was unavailing, for she was hit again and again by the monitor's guns and finally ran ashore. The Turks attempted to set fire to her, but we were able to re-capture her before this did much damage and the flames were extinguished. A British crew was put on board, the white Ensign hoisted and without further ceremony she reverted to her original owners and carried on. The *Pioneer* was now on fire and the next to be abandoned; all was not well with the Turkish Navy that day, for besides these ships we also captured ten barges, a number of pontoons and a large quantity of ammunition, rifles and general equipment.

The Navy was now far ahead of the Army in the pursuit and it was considered advisable to anchor here till the troops, who were still engaged in fighting rearguard actions, came up.

When our advance continued, two days after, our ships met with little opposition for some time, and arriving at Ctesiphon on March 6th they found the strong enemy position there deserted, but the day following they came under heavy fire from the Turkish guns on the North bank of the Dialah River, which joins the Tigris about eight miles below Baghdad. A brisk reply was given by the naval guns and this proved to be the last gasp of the retreating Turks, for during the night of March 10th-11th the position was evacuated and all hope of saving Baghdad was given up.

The following day the naval forces continued their advance without opposition from the now thoroughly routed Turks, and to the Navy belongs the honour of being first to take possession of the City of the Caliphs, for the Army Commander was borne there by water. The official account of Captain Nunn reads : " I arrived at the citadel at Baghdad in H.M.S. *Mantis* at 3.40 p.m., on Sunday 11th March. Paddle-steamer No 53, having on board General Sir S. F. Maude and staff, being in company with the flotilla."

So much for the facts, but behind it all is food for the imagination, for on this memorable day the Union Jack was hoisted over the famous City of Old Romance for the first time in the history of the world : many pageants had Baghdad witnessed in the old days of its splendour, but, I think, never one so wonderful as that which it saw this day; when the sea-power of a little island set far in the cold northern mists was felt and seen in this inland city, hundreds of miles from the coast, beneath the blue skies and flaming sun of the Orient.

CHAPTER XII.

THE MERCHANT SERVICE IN THE WAR.

IT would be unfair in a book on the Naval Front not to mention the Merchant Service, for no one stuck to their guns, literally as well as metaphorically, more pluckily than the men on our merchant ships.

" Both the Royal Navy and the Mercantile Marine are now one service in spirit," wrote Admiral Jellicoe, " and never have British seamen united in a more stern and mighty cause. Without our Mercantile Marine, the Navy—and indeed the nation—could not exist."

This is high praise from a famous Admiral, but it is nothing more than the truth, and when the full story of all the gallant deeds of the merchant service in the war comes to be written, as I hope it will be, the Empire will have a record of which she may well be proud.

As I have quoted the words of a great Admiral about these men perhaps those of a great civilian

—the Prime Minister—will also be of interest: " The officers and men of the Mercantile Marine," he said, " have won the distinction of being placed in the same category as the soldiers of the British Army and the sailors of the British Navy. Seamanship is at best a comfortless and a cheerless calling. What is it now ? During the war the strain, the hardship, the terror, the peril have increased manifold. Piracy is more rampant and ruthless than it has ever been in the history of the world. This is a new terror added to those of the deep. The risks of the navigator have increased in every direction. Lighthouses, which were there to warn the mariner against imminent peril, are, many of them, dark.

" They have to drive their ships full speed through fog and through storm, maintaining a ceaseless watch by day and by night, their eyes peering through the dark for objects hardly visible on the surface, even in sunlight, and yet life depends upon their observing these objects in time. Then when the blow comes from the invisible foe they are faced with conditions which would make the stoutest hearts pall. The mariner is left with the surging seas around him, scores of miles from a friendly shore : and yet amongst those who go down to the deep in ships there has not been found one man who failed to return.

"I have made enquiries, and I am told on all hands that the men return with greater alacrity than in times of peace—men torpedoed twice, thrice, seven times. They hardly wait for their papers before they return, because they realise that in these times their country cannot spare one man or one hour of time."

When Germany announced that on March 1st, 1916, she intended to start an " unrestricted submarine campaign," (although no one had noticed any particular restriction about it before this date) it was against merchant ships that this threat was more particularly levelled. The sinkings gradually increased, till the proportions became large, in spite of the vigorous counter measures that had been adopted against the U-Boats. The Hun liked sinking merchant ships, for in these days the majority of them were unarmed, and this sort of warfare suited his idea of fair play, but what the U-Boat feared most of all were the destroyers which usually formed the escort when the convoy system became more general. These boats, too fast to torpedo with any certainty and well armed with guns and that *bête noir* of the U-Boat, the depth charge, were the saviours of numbers of merchant ships, In spite of this it was not always possible for merchantmen to arrange to sail with a convoy, and it was these isolated vessels upon which the U-Boat used to prey, and many a plucky fight was put up by these ships before they were sunk, though on more than one occasion the tale was reversed and the attacker destroyed by gunfire or ramming, as in the case of *S.S. Wandle*.

The International Conference of Merchant Seamen has drawn up a report of authenticated cases of U-Boat commanders firing on survivors while in ships' boats and this list is a long one and a damning indictment of piracy and German savagery, which scoffed at every honourable tradition of sea-warfare. One can understand the German people being elated by the achievement of U-9 which sank the three British cruisers, *Aboukir*, *Cressy* and *Hogue* off the Dutch coast in September 1914. From their point of view this was a good piece of work, and of course a perfectly legitimate act of war, but that a nation could rejoice, as the Germans did so gloatingly, over the U-Boat murders gives one an insight into the mind of the Hun. The list of foul crimes to which the U-Boat commanders sank is too long to quote here, but I think the worst piece of cold blooded savagery was the action of U-55 in the case of *S.S. Belgian Prince*.

When this ship had been sunk the boats were broken up and the survivors, after being deprived of their lifebelts, were made to stand on the deck of the submarine which got under way and after a time submerged without warning, throwing those on deck into the sea and leaving them to their fate, which for twelve out of fourteen of them was death. I doubt if the annals of any war in the world's history contains so foul a stain on its pages, as this treatment of unarmed non-combatants by the German Navy.

The forces escorting merchant ships did not always escape without disaster, the most famous case perhaps being the fate of the destroyers *Mary Rose* and *Strongbow* when they were engaged in escorting a convoy of twelve neutral merchantmen between the Shetlands and the Norwegian coast on the night of Oct. 16th-17th,

Y

1917. They were attacked by two fast and heavily armed enemy raiding cruisers, but in spite of the unequal odds the two destroyers put up a plucky fight. Such a contest, however, could have only one end. The *Mary Rose* was the first to go, a shell hitting her magazine and blowing her up ; but the *Strongbow* fought on for over half an hour, though her wireless gear had been shot away and she knew that she could send out no call for assistance. Finally she, too, was sunk, with her colours still flying. All the crew of the *Mary Rose*, eighty-six, were lost and forty-six of the *Strongbow's* men.

The German cruisers then commenced to shell the unarmed merchantmen and sank nine of them, the other three managing to make their escape. Three H.M. trawlers were with the convoy and one of these, the *Elise* was successful in picking up twenty-nine survivors from the neutral ships, in spite of the heavy fire from the enemy.

As the convoy system increased in efficiency the sinking of merchant ships naturally became less. " Unless the weather is very favourable," wrote an officer who has had a great deal of experience in this work, " with low visibility

and a moderate sea breaking, or unless the convoy
contains large transports or other ships of exceptional value, the U-Boats hesitate to attack.
It has come to this, that a submarine can attack
most convoys with a fair chance of getting
one ship, but unless conditions are unusually
favourable the chances are that the price for
that ship will be the life of the submarine. A
periscope is hard to see and the U-Boat has a
fair chance of taking aim unobserved, but once
the torpedo is fired let it look to its safety. As
soon as the torpedo is seen three or four or seven
or eight destroyers, trawlers, or other convoy
guards will rush to the region from which the
" tin fish " came and begin dropping depth-
charges. By hydrophone or by the aid of oil
patches, which are the nightmares of all U-Boat
commanders, the Hun may be located accurately.
But if not, the destroyers are faster than he
and plaster with depth-charges the whole area
through which he might be trying to escape.
With the exception of one or two big prizes like
the *Leviathan*, the Germans seldom think one merchant ship worth the exchange of one submarine."

Germany has many stupid lies to her credit,
but perhaps she was never wider of the mark

than when, speaking through the mouthpiece
of a newspaper, the *Deutsche Tageszeitung*, she
said, " The submarine scare has struck England
with paralysing effect, and the whole sea is as
if swept clean at one blow." The man who
wrote these words could never have been in the
Downs during the war, where hundreds of ships
passed daily and a hundred more were at anchor
awaiting examination. All ports round the
United Kingdom could tell the same tale, most
of which were bustling with the activity of
arrivals and sailings. Supposing, for a moment,
that the German assertion was true, how did
they explain the fact that there were still British
ships to sink in waters widely apart ? But
then, I suppose, the Germans *don't* explain their
" facts " !

Sometimes the Hun was outwitted by other
means than fighting and perhaps the most
notable instance of this was the clever and very
daring manœuvre of *S.S. Ortega*, which was
described by the British Consul-General at Rio
Janeiro as " a most notable feat of pluck and
skilful seamanship."

The *Ortega* was a ship of some 8,000 tons
and in September 1914 she was on voyage from

South America to Liverpool; when near the
entrance to the Magellan Straits she encountered
the German cruiser *Dresden*, which was then
raiding commerce in these waters. The commander
of the *Ortega*, Lieut. D. R. Kinneir, R.N.R.,
at once realised that to continue on his course
through the straits was but to court disaster
in running right into the hands of the enemy,
and even to turn and run for it (for the merchantman was unarmed) would be no better, for the
Ortega's speed was only 14 knots against the
cruiser's 21. Lieut. Kinneir had on board his
ship 300 French reservists on their way to the
front, so it was imperative that he should do all
that was possible to save his vessel, and he
decided that the only thing to be done was to run
up the Nelson Strait, which lay on his port bow
and make an attempt to navigate the uncharted
and dangerous channel through the Queen
Adelaide Archipelago. In all the annals of the
sea it would be hard to find a more daring feat
than this. The waters were not only uncharted
but were strewn with reefs and rocks, and strong
unknown currents swept between its rocky sides
which rose in perpendicular walls on either side.
To attempt such a thing in normal times would

have been madness, for even the official charts of the ordinary route through the Magellan Straits and adjacent waters bear this notice: " Seamen are cautioned not to make free with these shores as they are very imperfectly known, and from their wild desolate character they cannot be approached with safety."

The Nelson Strait had never been attempted by a steamship before and it was a wonderful trial of skill and pluck against a powerful foe with modern guns that Lieut. Kinneir attempted that day. To hesitate was to be lost and to go on was very likely to be lost also. But he went on. As soon as the *Dresden* saw what the British ship was going to do she put on speed and chased her to the entrance of the Strait, firing as she came, but her shots fell short and the German captain dare not follow his intended victim into those dangerous waters and had the chagrin of seeing his quarry slip away out of range without being able to raise a hand to stop him.

The *Ortega* continued on her course, for the German ship was still waiting at the entrance to the Straits, never deeming that the British ship would carry on, but would be certain to turn back eventually : but the German captain reckoned wrongly, the *Ortega* never turned back from the dangerous passage. On and on the brave merchantman crept, at dead slow speed, with the lead constantly going and a sharp lookout from the crow's-nest. The luck of the brave was with the ship, for after anchoring at dusk, she continued the voyage at dawn, and finally came again, through the Smyth Channel, to Magellan Straits.

It was a great feat to have brought so large a ship through these rocky and uncharted seas, but it was a deed typical of the pluck and resource shown by the merchant service during the war.

It is said that those who watch and wait also fight, and it is equally true that those who carry on so splendidly in face of all perils fight as well as any. England can never forget the deeds of the Royal Navy in the great conflict, but let her remember also the doings of her Mercantile Marine, who likewise fought, and fought a winning fight against terrible odds.

CHAPTER XIII.

THE AMERICAN NAVY IN TIIE WAR.

I FIRST heard the news of the entry of America into the war in quite a dramatic fashion. We were out on a four days' patrol in the North Sea in the spring of 1917; it was a raw misty morning I remember, and we had just gone alongside an isolated lightship to give them some news-papers, when all at once out of the mist loomed a destroyer. Challenge and reply by searchlight morse followed, and apparently being reassured that we were not a Hun submarine—for an M.L. in a mist is not at all unlike a submarine—the destroyer sheered off to carry on her patrol. Just as she was disappearing again into the bank of fog her searchlight started morsing to us once more and this is the message that she flashed to us, " America has declared war." Our searchlight replied, " Good luck to her," and we disappeared from each other to depart on our respective vigils.

"AMERICA HAS DECLARED WAR"

Motor Launches on Patrol off the Newarp Lightship, learning the news by Morse from a passing Destroyer.

I immediately went below and woke up my First Lieutenant—at that time a Canadian—and, when I had convinced him that we were not in immediate danger of attack, I broke the news to him and we drank success to our new ally in a drop of hot " Nelson's Blood."

The sinking of the *Lusitania* is always quoted as the reason of America's entry into the war, and in a way this is true enough, but really it was but the spark that lit the fire that was already smouldering. The mind of every decent person in America had long been made up that it was her duty to take the only honourable course open to her and to declare war on the foe that had violated, not only the rules of war, but the rules of God and man as well.

The words used by President Wilson in his speech to Congress are now famous. It was America's duty, he said, to take up the challenge that the Germans had thrown down to the world in violating all laws of honour and liberty as she had done. " To such a task we can dedicate our lives and our fortunes," added the President at the conclusion of his speech, " everything that we are and everything that we have, with the pride of those who know that the day has

z

come when America is privileged to spend her blood and her might for the 'principles that gave her birth and happiness and the peace which she has treasured. God helping her, she can do no other."

The completeness with which America set about her war preparations as regards the Army is well known, but equally complete and speedy were her naval preparations. To give a detailed account of all these would take too long, but it will give some indication of the matter when it is said that although America's declaration of war took place only in April, by May a flotilla of their destroyers was operating in British waters equipped for long service away from their home bases.

Coming in as they did in the middle of the war to work with our Navy and under conditions entirely new to them, great credit is due to the American officers and men for the way they adapted themselves to new conditions. There was no friction, the Americans seemed to slide naturally into their place as part of the naval forces combined to fight the enemy.

I think, as I have to compress into one chapter that which would easily fill a book of its own, it will be best to give more or less in summary form the main activities of the American Navy operating in European waters or on convoy work.

The 6th Battle Squadron which operated with the Grand Fleet was composed of American battleships under Admiral Hugh Rodman, who flew his flag on the *New York*, the other ships being the *Florida*, the *Wyoming*, the *Delaware* and the *Texas*, with later on the *Arkansas*, relieving the *Delaware*. This Squadron took their place with others of the Grand Fleet in the various duties of the great northern base and on several occasions was assigned a place in the battle line when action with the enemy was expected.

There is no doubt that the Germans were very anxious to sink an American battleship; they thought the moral effect of such an act would be an asset to them. On several occasions the American Squadron was the subject of torpedo attacks. Early in February, 1918, the *Florida* and the *Delaware* while manœuvring off the coast of Norway while on convoy duty sighted a German submarine which fired four torpedoes at the *Florida* and two at her consort.

By skilful handling both ships managed to avoid being hit. The submarine disappeared after destroyers had dropped depth-charges. A couple of months later the *Texas* engaged a submarine which was about to attack them, but this also escaped. In the following June the American Squadron was again in action with enemy submarines. While proceeding to sea in open order line abreast a periscope was reported from the look-out on the *Wyoming* and soon after this was also seen by the *Parker*, one of the division of American destroyers that were operating with their battleships. The *Delaware*, *Florida* and *Wyoming* at once opened fire and the destroyers *Salmon*, *Parker* and *Radstock* dropped depth-charges. The submarine submerged at once, but reappeared about an hour later, when ten more depth-charges were dropped by the destroyers. Nothing more was seen of the U-Boat, but it was believed to be destroyed.

A month later a German submarine was rammed and sunk by the *New York* in the Pentland Firth. A U-Boat was known to be in the vicinity and had been engaged by the *Arkansas* a little earlier, and the *New York*, seeing a suspicious object in the water, at once altered

course to bring this ahead and put on full speed.
A heavy underwater blow was felt on the starboard quarter, followed almost at once by a
second, which broke two blades of the ship's
propellers.   Nothing more was seen of the submarine which must have sunk at once, never
to break surface again.   A few days later,
when on the way to refit after her damage the
New York had another narrow escape.   A submarine appeared suddenly and fired three
torpedoes at her in quick succession;   all these
passed ahead of the battleship, and there is no
doubt that the submarine misjudged the speed
of the American ship, which, on account of her
damaged propellers, was doing only 12 knots.

But in spite of all their efforts the Germans
were never successful in sinking any of the 6th
Battle Squadron during the two years that these
ships were operating in the North Sea.   This
squadron played their part, too, in the great
Pageant of Disgrace—the surrender of the German
High Seas Fleet, which, without striking a blow,
gave themselves up to everlasting ignominy and
shame.

Another division of U.S. Dreadnoughts was
based on the west of Ireland coast, where they

were held in constant readiness in the event of attack on convoys by any enemy cruisers or heavily armed ships. This squadron was under the command of Rear-Admiral T. S. Rodgers, who flew his flag on *U.S.S. Utah.*

The largest force of American destroyers operating on this side was based at Queenstown, under Admiral Sims. These efficient little ships were of the greatest service in the zone off the Irish coast which was a happy hunting ground for the submarine. The Americans came over at a time when the U-Boat menace was at its worst, and were a very welcome addition to our own over-worked destroyers which were operating in these waters. For hard work, length of time at sea and general utility the Queenstown destroyers of the U.S. Navy were certainly " right there."

Beside the Queenstown Base there were American destroyers stationed at Brest, Gibraltar and Plymouth all of which were engaged on escort work and patrol duty.

The general public has heard little about American submarines in the war zone, but seven operated from Berehaven and five from the Azores. These submarines patrolled convoy

lines and seriously hampered the operations
of the U-Boats, upon which four torpedo attacks
were made and in one of these, in July, 1918,
the A.L. 2 was successful in sinking U.B. 65.

One feat of which the American Navy is
justly proud is their share in the laying of the
Northern Mine Barrage, that huge mined area
that extended from the Orkney Islands to the
Norwegian coast. This area was approximately
250 miles long and 30 miles wide and consisted
of 15 strings of mines about 100 yards apart.
The work occupied about seven months and was
close to completion when the Armistice put an
end to hostilities. About eighty per cent. of
these mines were laid by a special flotilla of
American mine-layers.

Although it is hard always to tell the results
of such a minefield it is definitely known that
six U-Boats were destroyed in endeavouring
to cross this area, and it is very probable that
a good many more were accounted for, or at
any rate seriously damaged. That this great
barrage had a considerable moral effect upon
the crews of German submarines is now known
beyond question, for information has now come
from German sources of the panic caused in their

submarine flotillas, when the news of this new move on the part of the allied Navy became known.

The long voyage that was necessary before American troops could reach the war area meant not only a large number of transports but also a large number of escorting ships, and naturally a good part of this particular convoy work fell to the American Navy, and it certainly reflects high credit upon their zeal and efficiency when the vast number of troops carried those thousands of miles in safety is taken into account. The lion's share of escort duty fell upon the destroyers, although a certain number of cruisers were also employed.

An American author in one of their papers has written, " There will be millions of American soldiers after this war with a warm spot in their hearts for destroyers—those daring, nimble sea-hounds who hunt down the U-Boats and bring transports safely into harbour. An elderly Milwaukee American who crossed to France on an Army transport, wrote home to tell his son how well American destroyers had guarded him. He had never seen salt water before this voyage, and he was excusably confused on several

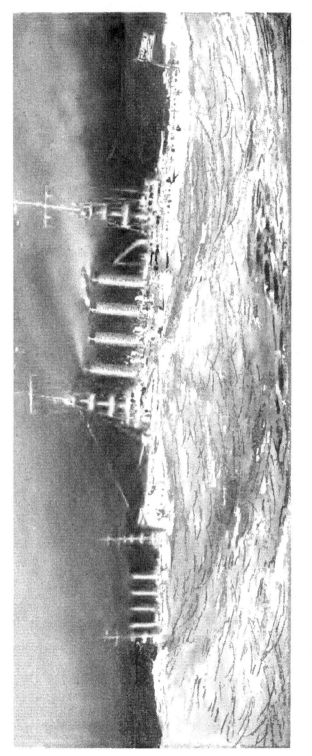

THE ATLANTIC FERRY
American Cruisers on Convoy Duty.

points. In particular, the characteristic quick
dashing, pitching, and rolling of destroyers with
a high speed convoy seem to have impressed
him, for he wrote : 'when we were a few days
from land four American destroyers met us and
began to fight off the submarines. Son, these,
destroyers are wonderful little boats. For three
days they were fighting U-Boats without a rest,
most of the time under water. Son, whenever
you meet any fellows from the American Navy,
take off your hat. They're *there.*'

" Unfortunately for our Navy, convoy duty is
not usually so exciting as this warm-hearted
patriot imagined. Most sea-duty, whether on
convoy or patrol, is a long, cold, wet, uneventful
grind, with little to keep the tiring mind to the
pitch of vigilance which must be maintained.
The Navy men see little romance in the work
now ; they will see that later when they look
back at it from the comfortable *ennui* of peace-
time routine."

And as one who has had a full share of both
patrol and convoy work I can fully endorse the
remarks of this American writer when he speaks
of the " wet, uneventful grind." There is little
pleasure on a winter patrol, especially at night,

but it was these " grinds " that kept the U-Boats away and allowed millions of men to reach Europe in safety.

To put this in figures, which, I suppose, are the things that tell, if plainly and without romance. In 1918 alone 1,895,805 American troops were transported to Europe, and of these about 60 per cent. were escorted by American destroyers, who also escorted nearly 30 per cent. of the cargo vessels for the same period.

America, like ourselves, had a fleet of Motor Launches. These boats were rather larger than our M.L.s being 110 feet to our 80, but carrying out practically the same work. These sub-chasers—as they were known officially—carried a crew of 2 officers and 23 men. Their armament was a 3″ gun, a Y gun (or depth-charge thrower), and a dozen depth-charges of a pattern very similar to our own type.

A hundred and twenty of these little craft crossed the Atlantic, by way of Bermuda and the Azores, in convoys of 12 to 24, as they were commissioned. The long voyage necessitated re-fuelling at sea and towing for part of the way. For this purpose special deep-sea tugs accompanied them.

They were based at Queenstown and Plymouth, while a flotilla was sent to the Mediterranean and operated from Corfu. Like our own M.L.s they were equipped with up-to-date hydrophones and all devices for outwitting the U-Boat.

Possibly their best performance, certainly the most spectacular one, was the share the sub-chasers took in the attack upon the Albanian harbour of Durazzo, where they were the covering force for the British and Italian ships which took part in the bombardment. The chasers came under very heavy fire from the shore batteries, but luckily without casualties, and were successful in foiling a submarine attack that was about to be made on the larger vessels. They sank one submarine by gun fire and depth-charges, and damaged another so severely that it is doubtful if it ever reached port. Subsequently they took part in the capture of Durazzo and, by sinking two mines at the entrance to the harbour just as a flotilla of British destroyers was coming along at high speed, probably saved many casualties.

It was an exciting and eventful day for the chasers and the commander of the British force in telegraphing his appreciation of their efforts to Admiral Sims finished with the significant remark, "They thoroughly enjoyed themselves."

Such is a very brief review of America's part in the Naval Front as regards the fighting ships, though a number of other vessels, such as oilers, tugs, tenders and such like were also in these waters. Altogether at the time of the armistice America had a total of 374 vessels of different sorts in various Naval Bases in Europe.

Nor did her naval activities end with the sea, for on the Western Front in France five trains of large calibre naval guns, manned entirely by sailors, were operating with the American Army ; while the American Naval Aviation Force established numerous bases both in Ireland and France, but the story of both these forces belongs to the land and air fronts rather than to the sea.

CHAPTER XIV.

THE SILENT VICTORY.

THE greatest naval victory the world has ever seen was achieved without firing a single shot. It was not the sort of victory the British Navy wanted, who, to a man, would have preferred to meet the enemy in open and fair fight at sea; but still no greater compliment could have been paid to the power of our Navy than this confession on the part of the enemy that they were afraid to come out and meet them, and preferred to suffer everlasting shame and humiliation by surrendering without a blow and coming to heel liked a whipped cur.

The remark of Admiral Sir Rosslyn Wemyss, in reply to the stupid boast of the German Admiral to the effect that the German Navy had not been defeated, is famous. Adjusting his eye-glass in his own particular way the British Admiral replied, " It only had to come out, sir." No finer or more crushing retort could have been

made to such a remark, made by a leader of a
fleet that had not shown itself outside harbour
for two and a half years.

The fleet that Germany had to hand over to
the British consisted, by the terms of the armistice, of ten battleships, six battle-cruisers, eight
light cruisers, fifty destroyers and all the U-
Boats that still remained in commission.

Over two hundred U-Boats had been sunk or
disabled by the allied Navies during the war
and the surrender of the rest began first. It
was found impossible to deliver all these at once,
some were under repair, and others in the Mediterranean.

The first instalment consisted of a batch of
twenty of these vessels; and early in the morning
of November 11th, 1918, the British force put
to sea from Harwich to meet them. Rear-Admiral
Sir Reginald Tyrwhitt led the British in his
flagship *Curaçoa*, with the light cruisers *Danae*,
Dragon, *Centaur* and *Coventry* and several
destroyers in attendance. Twenty miles from
the coast they met the U-Boats; all our men
being at action stations, for they had learnt by
long and bitter experience that the only German
that can be trusted is a dead one.

The long line of submarines, which were accompanied by two transports, were led shorewards to a spot a few miles outside the harbour, where the destroyers *Melampus* and *Firedrake*, and several M.L.s were waiting with surplus British crews to bring the surrendered ships into harbour. It was an unforgettable sight when the German ensign was hauled down, as each U-Boat was boarded by the captors, to go up again a minute later *under* the White Ensign. It seemed to repay, to some extent, all the dangers, hardships and long weary watches that we had been through during the four and a half years that lay behind.

One of the most impressive things about this surrender was the dead silence that prevailed among the thousands of spectators that lined the banks as the U-Boats came into harbour. Without demonstration of any kind these sea-murderers, who had fouled the name of the second largest Navy in the world with a stain that nothing can wash out, went to their captivity. There were no cheers and no jeers, for it is not the British way to hit a man when he is down, however big a cad he may be; but rather with a silent contempt and a loathing that was felt if not expressed, these foul things, with the blood of the innocent on their heads, passed to their eternal shame.

Their prison was the River Stour, just above the British submarine depôt at Parkeston Quay, where the U-Boats were moored at trots in a long double line, increasing in length as more boats came in, for it took over two months for all to surrender.

It had the appearance of a street, for it was over half a mile long, especially at night when the mooring lights added to the effect. "U-Boat Avenue," as it was known, where lay these emblems of "frightfulness," these sea-serpents with their fangs drawn, was a sight to make one think. It typified the sacrifice of a nation; on these submarines the Germans had spent millions and in their deeds the German people had put their faith. The British Navy was to crumble before their stab in the dark methods, Britain's commerce was to be dealt its death blow; but somehow with their usual obstinacy these "pig-dog Islanders" carried on just the same and merely adopted counter-methods that defeated the U-Boat—and now these vessels, once the hope of the German Nation, lay silent

U-BOAT AVENUE, HARWICH EVENING

By the courtesy of the Imperial War Museum

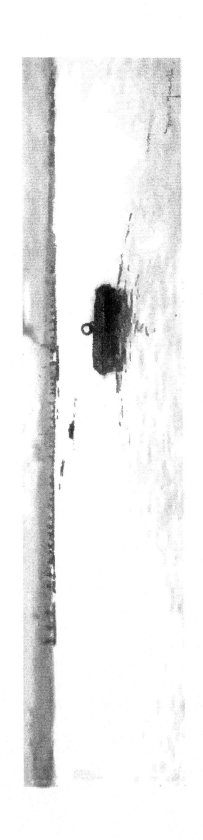

and deserted, captive in the hands of those very people they were built to destroy.

The surrender of the German High Seas Fleet took place on November 21st, the day after the commencement of the U-Boat arrivals. Long before dawn the Grand Fleet was in position off the Firth of Forth, and for nearly a hundred miles formed two great floating walls, between which the German ships were to steam, a fitting conclusion to the Naval War, for it was the iron wall that encircled Britain, through which the enemy was unable to pass, that won the victory for us.

Admiral Sir David Beatty was in command, flying his flag on the *Queen Elizabeth*, which led the surrendered ships down the lines. A British force consisting of light cruisers and destroyers had set out the night before and met the Germans at a rendezvous at sea and led them to the British Admiral who took the surrender. As in the case of the U-Boat surrender the men of the Grand Fleet were at action stations while the long line of enemy ships approached through the North Sea fog, which had hung about for several days, though the sun later on shone through the mists on to this historic spectacle.

The German Fleet that Sir David Beatty led down the British lines was itself led by its own Battle Cruiser Squadron consisting of the *Derfflinger, Hindenburg, Moltke, Von der Tann* and *Seydlitz*; the battleships followed, *Friedrich der Grosse*, flying the flag of the German Admiral, *Grosser Kürfürst, Kronprinz Wilhelm, Bayern, Markgraf, Prinz Regent Luitpold, Kaiserin, Kaiser* and *König Albrecht*. Astern of these were the light cruisers *Emden, Karlsruhe, Frankfurt, Bremen, Brummer* and *Nürnberg* (the *Köln* had turned back, having broken down en route), with the destroyers in five lines in the rear of all.

Thus the finest ships of the second largest Navy in the world tamely surrendered without striking a blow in their own defence, preferring this greater defeat than the one that would have been theirs had they chosen the honourable course—to come out and fight.

At sunset on this memorable day Admiral Beatty issued his famous signal to the German ships :

" The German flag is to be hauled down at 3.57 p.m. to-day, and is not to be hoisted again without permission."

WITH DRAWN FANGS

Surrendered U-boats by Moonlight at Harwich.

This signal, which will go down to posterity with that of Nelson before Trafalgar, was the final note in the death knell of Germany as a naval power.

The long watch and ward of the British Navy was over and the Naval Front was still as intact and unbroken as at the outbreak of war. As an island people this front was the most vital to us of all, our very life's blood depended upon this being held inviolate. To the Royal Navy the nation looked in its hour of peril, and the Navy was true to its trust.

INDEX OF PRINCIPAL NAMES.

All officers mentioned are R.N , unless otherwise stated.

PRINTED IN GREAT BRITAIN BY ROBERT MACLEHOSE AND CO. LTD , GLASGOW

CPSIA information can be obtained at www.ICGtesting.com
Printed in the USA
BVOW08s1200091214

378601BV00030B/748/P